Everyone knows leadership is changing. But being able to paint a dependable picture of the future of leadership isn't easy. And Clay Scroggins does just that. This is a book you'll want to keep close to you for a long time to come!

ANGELA AHRENDTS, former senior vice president of retail at Apple

A lively and refreshing take on what leaders must do in the days ahead. You will be challenged. You will laugh out loud. You will find yourself wanting to be a better version of yourself. Grab a copy and find a new bounce in your step.

CHERYL BACHELDER, former CEO of Popeyes Louisiana Kitchen and author of *Dare to Serve*

You can gain wisdom as a young leader in two ways. It can come to you as a gift, or you can gain it as some expensive lesson from a series of unfortunate mistakes. This book delivers wisdom as a gift. The insights in it will save you years of trial and error and countless costly mistakes.

CAREY NIEUWHOF, bestselling author of *At Your Best*

Leadership *is* changing. Clay does a tremendous job of describing the future of leadership in a practical, biblical, and entertaining way. As a leader who wants to help intentionally guide the future, I know I will put these principles into practice.

DAVE KATZ, president and chief operating officer of Coca-Cola Consolidated

THE
ASPIRING
LEADER'S
GUIDE
TO THE
FUTURE

THE
ASPIRING
LEADER'S
GUIDE
TO THE
FUTURE

9 SURPRISING WAYS
LEADERSHIP IS CHANGING

CLAY SCROGGINS

ZONDERVAN
REFLECTIVE

ZONDERVAN REFLECTIVE

The Aspiring Leader's Guide to the Future
Copyright © 2022 by Clay Scroggins

Requests for information should be addressed to:
Zondervan, *3900 Sparks Dr. SE, Grand Rapids, Michigan 49546*

Zondervan titles may be purchased in bulk for educational, business, fundraising, or sales promotional use. For information, please email SpecialMarkets@Zondervan.com.

ISBN 978-0-310-12445-0 (hardcover)
ISBN 978-0-310-12448-1 (international trade paper edition)
ISBN 978-0-310-12447-4 (audio)
ISBN 978-0-310-12446-7 (ebook)

Cover Design: Darren Welch Design
Cover Photo and Art: © *Svetlana-N/Shutterstock; Darren Welch*
Interior Design: Denise Froehlich

Printed in the United States of America

22 23 24 25 26 /LSC/ 10 9 8 7 6 5 4 3 2 1

Lucy, Jake, Sally, Cooper, and Whit: You're probably too young to enjoy this, but when you're old enough, I hope you'll choose to write your own. The world needs all our voices!

Contents

Acknowledgments

Boat loads of thanks to . . .

Ryan Pazdur and Kim Tanner for all the help on editing this book. This product is so much better than what I originally had. This section is the only thing you didn't make better, and I hope it's not super noticeable. Ha! Thank you.

Alexis De Weese and Jesse Hillman for helping with the plan on getting this message out to people. Writing the thing ain't easy, but getting it to people is just as hard. I'm so grateful for your hard work.

Suzy Gray and the North Point publishing team for the friendship, wisdom, and constant support.

Megan Gross for keeping all the plates spinning with excellence, kindness, grace, and humor.

Jenny for your belief in me. It is fuel to me. You simultaneously let me be me and make me want to be better. I love you so much!

CHAPTER 1

A New World Order

It was a Sunday night in October 1999, and I was headed to a meeting at Georgia Tech, where I was a student in industrial engineering.

I was late.

And so I did what people in 1999 did when they were running late.

I pulled over to a gas station, rummaged through the car seats to find a quarter, and used a pay phone to alert a friend of my tardiness. A pay phone. At a gas station.

Last week our family was headed to a friend's house, and we drove by that same spot. Different name but same station. And so I did what every nostalgic, always-looking-for-a-teachable-moment father does and took a minute to tell my kids the archaic story.

The main message to my kids? The world has changed drastically. Evolve or be left behind. Study in school, innovate, and create; don't spend your lives staring at screens.

Some leaders will be prepared and equipped for the future. Some won't.

In my own estimation, it was one of my better speeches.

No joke, their follow-up question was, "Dad, did the televisions have color back then?"

These twenty-first-century kids are savage. (Did I use that term correctly?)

As I told the story, I was reminded of the size of the chasm between the world I grew up in and the world they're navigating. They live their lives on their own devices, making their own calls, taking their own pics, and choosing what to watch, when they want to watch it, and whether it's good enough to finish.

In the case of the pay phone, it was a relic from the past that they could hardly fathom. If it weren't for our wildly interesting neighbor who has a replica of a red British phone booth in his front yard, our kids would've had literally no clue what a pay phone is. And when I say *literally*, I don't mean it figuratively, the way the kids are using it these days. I mean *literally* as in the way Webster defines it.

Clichés, Old Ways, and New Days

As I set out to research leadership today, I noticed that nearly every book, publication, article, and blog started with the same clichéd phrase:

Leadership is changing.

After seeing it about seventeen times, I heard a little sarcastic voice in my head, mocking the phrase: "Thanks, Sherlock. What else ya got?"

Of course leadership is changing. That's the easy part. The hard part is defining *how* it's changing. Can you identify the change? Are you able to see it before it gets here? Can and will you adapt? Do you have what it takes to become the leader the future is calling for?

Well, good news: That's why we're here, chugging through this book together.

I would never claim to know it all. I'm an engineering-trained, sermon-preaching, barbecue-loving golf hacker who happened upon a few opportunities to write about leadership. It's like Harry's wand. I didn't find the wand. The wand found me.

One thing I know to be true: no one knows the future. You should run the other way anytime anyone tries to convince you otherwise. All prognosticators are shooting in the dark, trying to find an empty wall where they can hang their dartboard. Also, if I could predict the future, I'm pretty sure I would use my talents on sports betting, stock trading, or political consulting.

All that to say, I certainly enjoy looking into the future. As an Enneagram Seven, I spend all my time looking out the windshield. I haven't exactly ripped off the rearview mirror, but mine is very small. My wife gives me a hard time because I have so few memories from my childhood. I loved growing up, but I spend much of my brain space looking out over the horizon of time. What's coming next? Where are we headed? What's it going to be like? Those are much more common questions for my wiring.

I'm convinced that my age also gives me a solid perspective on the future. Being born in 1980 puts me right on the edge of being a millennial and a Gen Xer. That unique perspective can serve as a bridge between two groups of people.

I'm young enough to remember life without the Internet. I distinctly remember the sound of dial-up internet, and I've both held a CD with AOL Instant Messenger on it and played Space Quarks on an Apple IIc. All of that happened while I was a teenager. Kids these days have never had to blow into Nintendo cartridges to clear out the fuzz, and it shows.

Though I'm not exactly a digital native, I'm close. I was a freshman the first year our university required students to own their own computers. That's not pay-phone old, but I can't imagine that schools include that requirement in the student handbook these days. My foreign language in college was not French, Spanish, or Mandarin. It was Java.

When it comes to leadership, I've been taking notes on the changes for a few decades now. My first *real job* was with Andersen Consulting, which soon after became Accenture. Working with a business strategy consulting firm during those years gave me a front-row seat to the dot-com boom and the subsequent dot-com crash. I'll never forget the day my roommate and I swung open the door to our room in our fraternity house and saw the display of groceries Webvan had just delivered. It was stunning. RIP, Webvan. The world wasn't ready for your greatness.

In the early 2000s, I watched a significant transfer of power as Sonny Perdue, the first Republican governor elected in Georgia since the 1800s, took office. And, yes, government work doesn't have a reputation of change, but the inherent transition of going from one party to another brought about quite a bit of change in and of itself. It also taught me that I didn't have what it takes to tackle that kind of work. You're welcome, Georgia.

I credit the majority of my leadership education to North Point Ministries and Andy Stanley. Of course, churches aren't exactly known for great leadership, but Andy is a one-of-a-kind leader. As long as I've worked for Andy, he's always told our organization, "This probably won't be the last job you have, but I want this to be the best job you've ever had. I want you to look back on this season and remember this as the best organization you've ever worked for." That's a high bar, but for me it's been true.

Andy and the team of people who manage our organization have built a culture of leadership. It's more common for us to pass around leadership books and articles than sermons and books on theology. Of course, there are those who feel that what we do is not spiritual enough, but our organization has chosen to believe that great leadership *is* a spiritual matter. If you've ever had a bad boss who seemed destined to bring hell to earth on a regular basis, you can understand why great leadership is "spiritual" work.

Over the past decade, I've been observing and prognosticating leadership, searching for a wall where I can hang up my own opinions about leadership and what it will look like in the future. Why? Because it matters. Who you are as a leader matters, but who you're *becoming* as a leader matters even more. Yes, of course leadership is changing. Drastically. And for you to become the kind of leader the future will demand, you have to see the changes, believe them, and change yourself.

No Bull's-Eye without a Target

We show new staff members a scene from the movie *Forgetting Sarah Marshall,* where Paul Rudd's character, Chuck, teaches Peter Bretter, played by Jason Segel, to surf. The scene creates some uncomfortable laughter for those who know the frustration of working in a job where the target keeps changing.

With Peter lying on the surfboard on the beach, an agitated Chuck spouts out these confusing orders: "I want you to ignore your instincts. Don't do anything. Don't try to surf. Don't do it. The less you do, the more you do. Let's see you pop up. Pop it up."

Peter tries, but stands up on the surfboard too quickly.

"That's not it at all. Do less. Get down. Try less. Do it again. Pop up."

Peter stands up more slowly, but evidently still too fast.

"No, too slow. Do less. Remember, don't do anything. Pop up. Well, you . . . No, you gotta do more than that, cause you're just lying right out. It looks like you're boogie-boarding."

Many of us know the aggravation of the target on the wall changing. When the target moves, it can be flat-out maddening. You climb the ladder through hard work, determination, and hustle, only for the boss to tell you the target has changed and your ladder is leaning against the wrong wall. That's why knowing what we're aiming toward is so important. When it comes to the leaders you and I are growing into, it's no different.

In leadership, clarity is kindness. The leaders we're most likely to follow are the ones who paint a picture of the future that's clear, attainable, and inspirational. Sadly, they don't even have to be great people. Plenty of dangerous leaders have done it with great skill.

Hitler did it.

David Koresh did it.

Heck, Adam Neumann, the founder of WeWork, did it.

Though predicting the future is nearly impossible, it's a necessary practice of great leadership. To be able to say, "This is what the future is going to be like," with some kind of certainty allows you and I to know where we need to develop and how we need to grow. We want to paint a

Bob Ross–esque picture of what leadership looks like in the future because it gives us something to aim for, work toward, and develop into.

I do this with my map app. Seriously. I need something to shoot for, which is why the map app is one of the top three most used apps on my phone. Even if I know how to get somewhere, I still input the address of the destination to see if I can beat the predicted time. It's a sick game I play to make me feel better about myself. And until you have to pay for a speeding ticket, it's free to play. Ha!

The GPS system our map apps use has taught me a simple principle:

<blockquote>
You're in a mess if you put the
wrong address in the GPS.
</blockquote>

Oh, that's right. I've got bars. (Mom, that's what the rappers are calling the lines they write these days.)

But seriously, you know how true that is. It's the same in life. In a society where we're consumed with personality surveys, temperament tests, and emotional awareness, understanding where we're headed is just as important as knowing where we are.

If you don't know the destination, you can't map a route to get there. And without a route, it's nearly impossible to know what steps to take along the way. It all starts with the destination. See it and you can start moving toward it. Miss it and you'll find yourself lost.

That's what this book is about. I hope to bring greater clarity to what you probably already know. You may not be shocked by the way leadership is changing, and, in fact, I bet you will be pleasantly surprised. I believe the driving forces causing these changes in leadership are steering us to a *better* way of leadership. As we see the future with more clarity, the way to get to the destination also becomes more clear.

So, yes, as clichéd as it is to say . . . leadership *is* changing. And it's changing in surprising ways.

New Leadership, New Skills

I noticed one way leadership is changing in a recent interview I did with Angela Ahrendts.

Angela is a force. An inspiring, bright, thoughtful, and impressive leader, Angela has a history of success. When she took over as CEO of Burberry in 2006, the company was growing at only 2 percent a year. But by 2012, Burberry's revenues and operating income had doubled over the previous five years.[1] The turnaround she maneuvered at Burberry is still one of the most remarkable case studies in digital transformation, brand repositioning, and culture overhaul. After an incredibly successful seven-year run at Burberry, Angela raised eyebrows in 2013 when she announced her acceptance of the role of senior vice president of retail at the largest tech giant in the world: Apple. They sell quite a bit of stuff at Apple, you know.

Think of how intimidating it would be to join Apple's C-suite leadership team. Fortunately, Angela strikes a great balance between confidence and humility. After starting her new job, one of the first moves she made to unify the seventy thousand Apple retail employees she oversaw was to send out simple videos shot from her office at the Apple headquarters in Cupertino. She called these Monday morning videos "Three Points in Three Minutes."

About one minute into the first and only take of her first Monday morning video, Angela's phone rang. It was her college-aged daughter, calling from London. Angela looked at the camera operator and quickly said, "Just keep rolling. This will be quick."

Then she picked up the phone and said, "Hi, Angelina. I'm recording this video, but I'm almost done. I'll call you right back."

She set the phone back down on her desk and picked right back up with the video. After finishing that take, she instructed the slim production crew, "Let's use that take just like that. Keep the phone call in it."

I believe this incident illustrates one of the changes we're seeing with a new kind of leader—someone willing and able to show vulnerability. The authenticity Angela displayed in taking the call from her daughter seems simple enough, but it communicated something profound to her employees: "I'm a real person. I manage the tension of the demands of personal life as well. I'm trying to be a great parent and spouse while also embarking on this journey to change people's lives through the products and services of our work. And it's possible to do both."

Do you desire to follow that kind of leader?

Do you desire to *become* that kind of leader? I sure do.

As iconic as the Apple logo is, and as great a reputation as the company has for innovation, uniting employees and teammates is not enough. Yet Angela's surprising moment of authenticity made an indelible mark on many Apple employees. "The next day I must have gotten five hundred emails of people thanking me for taking my daughter's call."[2] And Angela's actions gave her an opportunity to extend an invitation for others to join her. "I'm not a king or a queen or a dictator. I'm here to do my life's greatest work. Will you help me? Can we do it together?"[3]

The New Math of Leadership

The world is changing far too fast, information is exploding at an absurd rate, and communication is happening more rapidly than it ever has before. According to the World Economic Forum, the amount of data generated each day is staggering.

- 500 million tweets are sent.
- 294 billion emails are sent.
- 4 petabytes of data are created on Facebook.
- 4 terabytes of data are created from each connected car.

- 65 billion messages are sent on WhatsApp.
- 5 billion searches are made.

By 2025, an estimated 463 exabytes of data will be created each day. That's the equivalent of 212,765,957 DVDs per day.[4]

In a world of relentless change, the thought of being left behind is scary. The alarming potential that I might become as outdated as a Blockbuster video store motivates me to adapt. But it's not just my fear of becoming a fossilized leader; it's the reality of the ongoing technological revolutions and the implications these changes have for the workplace and our homes. Sure, we want to be known as great leaders, but downloading and installing a new leadership operating system feels like a chancy endeavor. Still, in light of our changing world, staying the same may be the greater risk.

Whether you have kids or not, you've probably heard parents complain about something called "new math." I remember helping our nine-year-old son with his long division, and immediately I knew he was doing it all wrong. Sure, the numbers were the same, but his process was entirely backward. Instead of working from right to left, as I was taught to do, he worked from left to right. I've taken a lot of math classes in my life, but my head hurt from trying to help him divide 645 by 15. I finally had to surrender and hand it back to him.

You might not feel motivated to learn new math. I sure don't. But we must find the motivation to learn new leadership. A calculator will do math, but it won't lead for us. We have to be able to see the changes on the horizon, identify the skills needed to adapt to those changes, and do the work of becoming a new kind of leader.

Where Leadership Is Going >
Where Leadership Has Been

If you're a leader (and you're a leader whether you realize it or not), you're in the fight of your life. The easy solutions don't work. (I've tried them.) The ground keeps shifting. And the target isn't exactly steady either. I'm convinced nothing is more difficult than leading because there's just no manual for it.

Sometimes we need a Zack Morris moment. In the television show *Saved by the Bell*, Zack often calls a time-out, and the action pauses while he talks directly to the camera. We need something like that—a pause to evaluate where we are, where we want to go, and how we're getting there.

My hope is that this book will create a port for your leadership, because fixing your boat while you're out at sea is too difficult. This is a chance to bring the ship into port, to think about the future. Thinking ahead is what guided Wayne Gretzky in his illustrious career: "I skate to where the puck is going to be, not where it has been."

I hope that reading this book will give you a moment of pause, for the sake of your future and for the sake of future generations.

CHAPTER 2

You Don't Have to Know It All to Start Leading

I graduated from the Georgia Institute of Technology with a degree in industrial engineering. That surprises people, for many reasons.

For one, I'm a pastor now. I can't say that my industrial engineering degree prepared me for the speaking and leadership roles I find myself in today. In fact, I had zero input on the layout of our church buildings, even though by virtue of my background and education, that's the one time our senior leadership should've asked for my opinion.

Second, Georgia Tech is an incredible school full of really smart people, and I don't quite fit the bill. No one who meets me walks away and thinks, "Wow, that Clay Scroggins sure seems book smart." And they would be right in that assessment. I was good enough to graduate from a challenging college, but I'm substantially more comfortable speaking in a large group gathering than studying in a library cubicle.

I've always been this way. I love to learn and grow and challenge myself, for sure. I love reading books and listening to people who are way smarter than I am, talking about topics they're well versed in. But I wasn't the kid on the dean's list every semester.

When I entered a leadership role, armed with keys to leadership I learned from books in university, I had plenty of moments when I thought, "Did I read the wrong books? Did I miss a class somewhere?" Leadership in practice is so different from what I thought it would be.

Part of the disconnect I've always felt with school is the idea that the purpose is to prove what you know. School is about providing the correct answers to questions and showing you've thought about something the correct way. It can be frustrating because that's not how real life works. There isn't always a correct answer or a right way. Comedian John Mulaney says it this way:

> In elementary school, it doesn't matter what you think. It just matters what you know. You have to have answers to questions, and if you say, "I don't know," you get an X on your test and you get it wrong. And that's not fair because your brain has never been smaller. Also, that's not how life works. If you came to me now and were like, "Hey, John, name three things that the Stamp Act

of 1765 accomplished," I'd go, "I don't know, get out of my apartment."

But when you're a little kid, you can't say, "I don't know." You should be able to. That should be an acceptable answer on a test. You should be able to write in: "I don't know. I know you told me. But I have had a very long day. I am very small. And I have no money. So you can imagine the kind of stress that I am under."

Real life is nothing like school. For one, in the real world, no one expects you to know everything. People don't walk up to you and ask about the Stamp Act of 1765. Even in the responsibilities of your job, there are things you don't know.

But admitting you don't know everything can be very hard to do.

"I Don't Know"

The idea that we need to *know everything* can easily sneak into our everyday lives, and this is especially true in leadership. There's a common misconception that the person (or people) at the top knows everything, or at least they know more than anyone else. For those of us hoping to be great leaders, we are under no illusions that we have all the answers. Yet there's an intense pressure to avoid admitting our lack of knowledge. We don't want to confess that we don't know everything.

But leading in the future will require saying those three simple words—*I don't know*—and saying them over and over again.

Those words aren't easy to say, are they? But why? In an insightful article, Dave Mayer, professor of business ethics at the University of Michigan, said, "Issues around confidence and competence fit into our prototype for what it means to be an effective leader."[1] He goes on to explain the idea of "implicit leadership theory," which is based on the idea that everyone has preconceived notions of how things should be, and we project those concepts onto our surroundings. So as we think about leadership, we all have subconscious ideas of what a leader *should* be that shape how we respond to people in positions of power.

Mayer goes on to explain that those ideas don't reflect "what actually is an effective leader. This is what people think is the stereotype or prototype of an effective leader. Some of the strongest parts of it have to do with things like being intelligent and being decisive. So when we picture a leader, we picture someone who has the right answer."[2] The irony is that some of the most effective leaders are those who flip these preconceived notions upside down. For example, many people have an implicit bias that assumes leaders are strong and powerful, yet in reality people are more likely to follow a leader who shows grace and exhibits humility.

This tendency also applies to the knowledge a leader

possesses, or at least the way they project themselves as competent and knowledgeable. Any leader can pretend by exhibiting a sense of confidence even when they don't know what they are doing, but the most influential leaders, according to Mayer, are those who "realize other people have insights and abilities that they might not."[3] This ability to *acknowledge our own lack of knowledge* opens the door to becoming better leaders, better communicators, and all-around better people.

Professionals at Pretending

Don't be a pretender. Though it may be tempting to act like you know what you are doing all the time, the truth is that you work against yourself when you pretend that you know something when you really don't. Yet many of us do this regularly out of fear of looking dumb or incompetent. I know I do! Our church regularly hosts a conference for church leaders all around the world. Hundreds of incredible men and women come to our church to ask us questions about how we do this or that and why we do what we do and what makes this ministry work. I never want to say to them, "I don't know." Never. These people have come to us looking for solutions, and giving them anything less than a confident, assured answer feels wrong. So even when I have no idea how a certain program works, when put on the spot, I always want to appear like I do.

The Aspiring Leader's Guide to the Future

In an episode of the *Freakonomics* podcast, Steven Levitt explored this compulsion we feel to appear intelligent in the business world:

> What I've found in business is that almost no one will ever admit to not knowing the answer to a question. So even if they absolutely have no idea what the answer is, if it's within their realm of expertise, faking is just an important part. I really have come to believe that one of the most important things you learn as an MBA is how to pretend you know the answer to any question even though you have absolutely no idea what you're talking about. And I've found it's really one of the most destructive factors in business—that everyone masquerades like they know the answer and no one will ever admit they don't know the answer.[4]

We see this behavior not only in business leaders. Politicians do it all the time too. Everything they say and do is an effort to convince you, the voter, that they know the answer. Otherwise, who's going to vote for the person who doesn't know what they're doing? Politicians lean into our implicit leadership biases by projecting confidence that they know best. And who can blame them? Their entire job is built on the premise that they know more than their constituents, that they're confident in what they know, and that they're able to clearly communicate what they know. Of course, that clear communication part rarely seems to happen these days, but oddly all this does is further the illusion that those in charge are smarter than the rest of us and that we—the plebeians— just don't get it.

Levitt goes on to highlight the problem with all of this pretending to know the answer: "It makes it almost impossible to learn."[5]

Politics and Leadership

All this pretending is unsustainable. Future leadership will flip this inability to admit ignorance on its head. We see this at work every day as leadership becomes more about authenticity—being someone real and true—and less about being blindly trusted as a so-called authority. This shift toward authenticity can be understood with a clear, though likely controversial, example: Alexandria Ocasio-Cortez.

Set aside your political preferences for a second and consider this. Ocasio-Cortez graduated from Boston University in 2011 with a bachelor of arts degree in both international relations and economics. She then moved back to the neighborhood where she grew up and worked as a server and bartender until running for Congress and getting elected in 2018.

Now compare her with another politician from the same party who represents a district roughly the same size. Former Congressman Dan Lipinski received a bachelor of science in mechanical engineering from Northwestern University, a master of science in engineering-economic systems from Stanford University, and a PhD in political science from Duke University. He served eight terms as the US representative for Illinois's Third Congressional District from 2005 until 2021.

Ocasio-Cortez and Lipinski both represent districts with a population of roughly seven hundred thousand people, but that may be the only thing they have in common. The reach and influence of these two politicians could not represent a greater contrast. Ocasio-Cortez has over 12.7 million Twitter followers, was named one of *Time* magazine's one hundred most influential people of 2019, was featured on the cover of *Vanity Fair*, and raised over $17 million in a reelection campaign that saw her win easily. Lipinski, on the other hand, has under twenty thousand Twitter followers, stayed more or less out of the public eye in his sixteen years in Congress, and lost his latest reelection campaign to entrepreneur-turned-politician Marie Newman.

I'm not suggesting that the number of Twitter followers has anything to do with someone's leadership capabilities, but it does tell us something about how well a person is able to capture the attention and support of large groups of people. Lipinski has a PhD in political science. That educational training should surely trump Ocasio-Cortez's bartending career, right? Yet it is Ocasio-Cortez, not Lipinski, who has become the face of the modern

Democratic Party. What does that tell us about the type of person people are looking for in a leader?

At the very least, it suggests that people today want accessibility and authenticity from those they follow. Few modern politicians have been able to speak the language of the people as fluently as Ocasio-Cortez, which serves as a reminder that leaders are more than degrees and past accomplishments. People want to follow someone who shares life with them, not just to trust someone based on their level of knowledge and past achievements.

Ocasio-Cortez's lack of experience has not hurt her appeal—oddly enough, it may even have helped. She has always been open about who she is, where she comes from, and what her experience (or lack thereof) has been. Many people are drawn to this level of honesty. Regardless of what you think of her politics, she has tapped into something many leaders neglect: *an integrity quotient.*

Are You Who You Say You Are?

Leadership gets tricky and dangerous if you believe that to lead you need to have all the answers. You will eventually find yourself in a situation where you don't have the answers and will either compromise the trust you've built (by lying or acting like you know what you're doing when you don't) or feel inadequate and quit ("I don't know; therefore, I can't lead").

But you can't fake people out forever. They know that leaders are human and don't always have the right answers. And when people look at a leader, they want to know what they're getting. That's what I mean by having an integrity quotient.

Typically, when we hear the word *integrity* we think *honesty*. The two words are often synonymous; a person of integrity is usually defined as one who tells the truth. But I want to consider a slightly different definition of *integrity*: the state of being whole and undivided. Someone who has integrity is consistent. Their thoughts, words, and actions are in alignment.

People want honest leaders, of course, but what they really want are leaders they can trust implicitly. And as strange as it may seem, admitting what you don't know is one of the fastest ways to build trust.

Tom Rath and Barry Conchie are the coauthors of *Strengths-Based Leadership*. In an interview, they described the importance of trust and consistency in leaders:

> **Tom Rath:** I think trust is primarily built through relationships, and it's important because it's the foundational currency that a leader has with his team or his followers.
>
> **Barry Conchie:** A baseline level of trust exists at the transactional level when people see leaders doing what they say they will do. But real trust is actually much more complicated

than that. Trust also speaks to behavioral predictability. It's hard to trust a volatile leader in times of change.[6]

When you lead with integrity, you remain consistent with who you are. Your identity is exhibited in the way you speak and act. This doesn't mean you need to be perfect, free of failure and mistakes. It doesn't mean you know everything. Rather, it means that when you don't know something, people trust you to admit it and act in a way that is worth following.

People want a leader who will always tell the truth. But what if you don't always know the truth? Then what do you say? Imagine a situation where an employee comes to you and says, "Are we going to meet our financial goals this quarter?" Perhaps the answer to that question, based on the information you possess at the time, is most likely no. Which answer do you think most people would rather hear in response:

"Probably not, no."
    or
"I don't know, but we're going to do everything we
    can to try."

The first one is honest. The second, though it admits ignorance of the future, inspires hope. People want a leader who admits what she doesn't know but will still try to do the best for the people around her. So if you are waiting for the day when you'll have all the answers to start leading, you'll be waiting forever. Remember: great leaders don't have all the answers, but they are honest and consistent, even when they don't know what the future holds.

Why does this matter to you today? Because you need to develop the kind of character today that will make you a better leader tomorrow.

The Patience of Fishermen

Jesus had twelve disciples. At least four of them were fishermen—Andrew, Peter, James, John. I don't know where fishing ranks on your list of hobbies, but it's not on mine. I'm not patient enough. A large part of fishing is faithfully showing up every morning (especially early in the morning, which is not something I associate with a fun hobby) and throwing in line after line, hoping to get a bite. I don't think it's coincidental that Jesus chose a group of fishermen to be his disciples.

What Jesus's disciples didn't know is that their entire lives had been leading up to the moment when they would encounter the living Son of God for the first time. Jesus didn't choose disciples who had strong religious backgrounds. He chose disciples who were ready to be faithful followers. Think of their profession and then consider what following Jesus required of them:

Fishing	Being a Disciple of Jesus
Wondering what each day would hold, how many fish they may or may not catch	Following Jesus from town to town, never knowing what he planned to do next
Being in the lower half of the social pecking order (fishing was a rough trade in biblical times)	Constantly being rebuked by religious leaders, chased out of cities, and shunned by general society
Knowing that success depended on faithful consistency and showing up in the boat day in and day out	Being faithful to a man who had come to save the world and showing up at his side day in and day out

As fishermen, Jesus's disciples lived with uncertainty, were on the outskirts of the social order, and understood the value of faithfulness and consistency. Whether they knew it or not, God had prepared them for the roles he had selected for them from the beginning of time. Their lives as fishermen prior to following Jesus were not wasted. They weren't simply counting down the days until "their time" came.

Sadly, many men and women today sit in their current career roles twiddling their thumbs, waiting for what's next. But God doesn't *waste* time. He's not behind schedule in setting up the leadership role he has planned and prepared for you. He has you where you are today for a reason. Maybe you don't think you know everything you need to know or don't feel like you have the experience you need to have, but that doesn't mean you are wasting your life. Join what God is already doing, and use the time you have now to start becoming the leader you want to be in the future.

Think about the characteristics of leaders you admire, and incorporate what they say and do into your own life. Faithfully and consistently develop your character so that when you are in a position of leadership and find yourself facing a situation with many unknowns, you know how to respond.

This all sounds a lot easier than it is. There are several character traits you could work on, putting into practice each day, so how do you decide where to start? That's where the three magic words come in: "I don't know."

You may not be able to practice leading a board meeting right now. But you *can* practice leading in other areas of life, even when you don't know everything. Try a new hobby, learn a new skill, and then try teaching it to someone else. You'll (hopefully) never know less than you do right now. So that means now is the perfect time to practice. I'm reminded of the well-known quote attributed to Abraham Lincoln: "I will study and get ready and someday my chance will come." Lincoln didn't wait until he had achieved the position of president to start preparing for the role. He spent many days of his life getting ready.

The Haves and Have-Nots

Experience and education can be great assets in life, and I'm all for equipping yourself and going to school, but keep in mind that these advantages can also exacerbate the trap of feeling like you know it all. If you have the doctorate or the experience that makes you qualified to lead, that's great! Work on becoming self-aware enough to acknowledge that those merits don't give you all the answers. If you are conscious of that, your education will help you rather than hinder you. I'm willing to bet that if you picked up a book on the future of leadership, you already realize that you don't know everything. So congratulations, you're already on the right track!

Recognizing that you don't know it all doesn't mean you shouldn't try to learn more. Consider that some of the best coaches in sports history were below-average players. Nick Saban, Bill Belichick, Bear Bryant, Dabo Swinney, Gregg Popovich—none of them were superstar athletes. But you want to know what all these guys were doing while they played? Learning.

You may have all the experience and knowledge you need to take the next step in your journey toward being a leader. You may have none of it. Your action items for today are the same regardless: develop integrity and consistency, understand that you don't have to know everything, and recognize that where you are right now is likely the best training ground to prepare you for where you want to be.

Becoming a leader isn't something that magically happens when you feel ready or suddenly know everything. It's the fruit of consistently making choices that reflect integrity, demonstrate authenticity, and exhibit patience with the process. Remember, it's okay to say, "I don't know." The best leaders do it all the time. Rather than sitting around waiting for a leadership opportunity to arrive, faithfully move forward with what you already have.

CHAPTER 3

Even the GOATs Will Have a Coach

It's the spring of 1997. The Spice Girls have just released their debut single, "Wannabe." A young man by the name of Leonardo DiCaprio is in the studio filming *Titanic* alongside Kate Winslet. And in the small town of Augusta, Georgia, Tiger Woods has won his first career Masters Tournament, setting records for lowest score to par and the largest margin of victory (twelve strokes) in tournament history.

After that huge win and at that point in his early career, Tiger Woods had won 21 percent of the PGA Tour events he entered and 25 percent of the majors he attended. His historic win at Augusta had a feeling of inevitability to it—it was never a matter of if, but when. By the end of that season, Tiger had won two more PGA events and received the title of PGA Player of the Year. Needless to say, his golf game was in pretty good shape.

Then he decided to change his swing.

Where I grew up, we had a saying: "If it ain't broke, don't fix it." Well, Tiger either hadn't heard that phrase or chose to ignore it. Either way, he was taking a huge risk in turning to legendary golf coach Butch Harmon for a swing change. Apparently, Tiger believed that "his club shaft was across the line at the peak of his backswing, with his clubface closed."[1] Whatever that means.

Harmon said he agreed with Tiger's self-assessment, but he wanted to fix the problems one piece at a time. He warned Tiger that this type of adjustment would likely make him less competitive on tour and advised Tiger to consider taking the year off if he was going to pursue such a sweeping change to his game. In typical fashion, Tiger rejected that plan, insisting they fix it all at once.

Well, Butch Harmon was right . . . kind of. In 1998 Tiger won only once, leading many journalists to question whether his success had been a flash in the pan. Would Tiger be a lightning strike—one flash of brilliance and then gone forever? Well, we now know the ending to this story. But the bounce back came about faster than you might have guessed.

The next year (1999), Tiger Woods won eight tournaments, including the PGA Championship. And the year after that, he won nine—including a record-tying six tournaments in a row, including the US Open, the Open Championship, and the PGA Championship yet again. Also, at that year's US Open, he broke or tied nine tournament records before becoming the youngest golfer to achieve the career Grand Slam (winning all four major tournaments). He was named *Sports Illustrated*'s Sportsman of the Year, becoming the first person to receive the award twice and the only person besides LeBron James to hold that claim. And if that wasn't enough, he went on to win the 2001 Masters, making him the only player ever to win four consecutive major golf titles.

He was unstoppable. PGA Tour events were suddenly where the best golfers in the world came to compete for *second* place. It wasn't a question of beating Tiger—it was a question of keeping it close. Since that time in the late nineties, Tiger's career has had more than its fair share of ups and downs. But for a time he was untouchable, the undisputed greatest of his time and arguably the GOAT—the greatest of all time.

And all this after turning to his coach and asking him to help fix a swing that wasn't broken.

Hungry Humility

On the surface, Tiger's story provides a unique example of humility. Seen by many as someone at the peak of his career, Tiger not only listened to the advice of his coach—he asked for it. Harmon has repeatedly referred to Tiger as "a sponge," implying that he sought counsel and input, always looking for ways to improve his game. He found a mentor. He asked questions. He listened to advice. Of course, Tiger wasn't an apathetic follower. He didn't blindly listen to whatever Butch Harmon had to say. But he welcomed the ideas of others, even though he was one of the best in the world.

I'm always encouraging people (young men in particular) to find a mentor—someone older, wiser, and more experienced who can guide them through life. But like many things we know we should do, we sometimes make being mentored another box we check off. Seeking out a mentor is more than asking someone, "Will you be my mentor?" That alone is not enough. If you want the most from a mentor, you need to put some thought into what you want beforehand. What do you want from a mentor? What's the purpose, the goal of getting together?

A great mentor-mentee relationship has defined rhythms and expectations. Finding a mentor or coach requires not only humility but also a hunger for something more. Humility says, "I can't do this alone, and I need the help of someone who knows better than I do." Hunger says, "This is the mountain I want to climb, and I want to do what it takes to get there."

Tiger didn't simply go to Harmon and say, "Will you fix my swing?" He had an idea of what he wanted. He said *this* is what I want to fix, and *this* is how I want to fix it. His goal wasn't simply to win; it was to dominate. And Tiger knew he needed help to get there. Tiger's humility in combination with his hunger and drive to win sets his story apart. He wanted his golf swing to look perfect while he dominated. And getting there required him to know himself—both his strengths and his weaknesses. Aspiring future leaders will have a good gauge on both of these, knowing where they are strong and where they are weak and need help to grow.

Think of a mentor as a fly-fishing guide. If you gave me a rod, a reel, and some flies, I could go out and catch fish. I could. It might take me a few days before I caught my first one, but I could do it with enough trial and error. I'd eventually figure it out and find the right place to catch something. But why *wouldn't* I hire a guide, someone who knows the river intimately, to tell me where to go? No one thinks less of someone who hires a fly-fishing guide. That's what you're supposed to do. That's *how* you find the fish—you ask someone who knows. The same is true for young leaders seeking a life coach.

While the need for a guide may seem self-evident to many of you, I emphasize it because there is a false notion that asking for help is a sign of weakness. Well, it isn't. The real sign of a weak leader is *not* asking for help. When you think you can do it alone, you're delusional, kidding yourself that you are wiser, smarter, and better than you really are. If the GOAT—the greatest of all time—needs a coach, it's a good bet you need one too. But there are two contrasting vices you'll need to overcome before coaching will be of help to you.

I Can Do This on My Own

When I was talking with a friend the other day, he shared his experience of going to counseling. Like many people, I have long held the wrong-headed idea that counseling is only for people who have experienced something really bad in life or are going through something exceptionally hard. So I was curious to learn why this friend—someone I know very well and who didn't seem, at least on the surface, to have a ton of issues to work through—was seeing a counselor. And so I asked him: "Why are you seeing a counselor?"

His answer was surprisingly simple: "Because my counselor wants to help me." That's it. There were no earth-shattering revelations. He told me this was the one hour each week when he could talk to someone about the good and the bad, about what was going well and what wasn't, and this person just listened, offering counsel where they could. Now, I'm not suggesting a coach is a fill-in for a counselor, as if these roles are interchangeable. But I think something about my friend's attitude toward counseling is helpful.

I was struck by the fact that *he felt no shame in seeing a counselor.* He wasn't trying to work through some deep, dark secret or terrible trauma. He just wanted help. For some reason, for many leaders (and aspiring leaders), asking for help isn't always seen as acceptable. We are conditioned—especially in Western leadership culture—to do everything on our own. We're told that success in life is about our performance as individuals and that it all depends on honing our own capabilities and overcoming our limitations.

But that's not true. Not only is this thinking antithetical to God's design for his church, but it works against our identity as individuals created in God's image. Any healthy society or culture is more than a collection of isolated individuals. It's easy for me to point this out and for you to nod your head in agreement (I don't assume you're actually nodding your head along with me, but maybe internally). But it's not easy to overcome the cultural pressures and to make asking for help a normative practice in our lives.

No one wants to acknowledge their weaknesses, let alone say them aloud. But your weaknesses will hold you back if you keep them to yourself. We were not designed to take care of ourselves apart from others. Shout-out to the garden of Eden: "Then the LORD God said, 'It is not good that the man should be alone; I will make him a helper fit for him'" (Genesis 2:18 ESV).

When God made the world, everything he made was *very* good, except for one thing—Adam was all alone. If you're going through life alone right now, trying to do it all on your own, you're not living out God's design, and you can probably sense that something is off. While this passage speaks directly of the relationship between a husband and wife, it's about more than that. In the New Testament, the apostle Paul constantly preached about the body of Christ, emphasizing that God's vision for his people is one of unity in committed relationships with others, seeking to honor God together. That's what we were made for!

I have no doubt that Tiger Woods would still be a good golfer even without the help of Butch Harmon. But I'm grateful that he asked for help because we were able to witness something better than good—we all got a taste of greatness. And I have no doubt that you are a good leader. Bad leaders don't read books on leadership. But I know you can be more than a good leader. You can be a great leader *if* you invite someone to help.

Maybe you still think you can become a great leader on your own. If so, good luck. Prove me wrong. Even if you do, I can guarantee you will become exhausted in the process. So ask yourself, "Why *not* ask for help? Why *not* share my weaknesses with someone who can help me sharpen them? Why *not* lean into the design that is woven into my very being?"

Seriously. Why not?

I Don't Really Want to Do This

Ah, yes. The flip side. Let me go ahead and answer that last rhetorical question for you: "Why not ask for help?" Well, the generic answer is, "Because I don't want to." Straight up, that's a fair answer. Getting a coach requires time, effort, and patience. From that list, I'm already short on number one, number two comes and goes, and my wife tells me number three sometimes disappears entirely. Laziness is a reasonable and realistic response. But it's also . . . well, lazy.

While I was in college, I studied abroad in Oxford, England, for a summer. It always tickles me to subtly drop that low-key flex in conversations because the truth is that there was no academic requirement to be accepted into this program. If there had been even the most minimal requirements for acceptance, I certainly would have been denied.

My favorite weekend excursion was to play golf in Scotland, the motherland of golf. On back-to-back days, my friends and I played two courses—the Old Course at St. Andrews and the Nairn Golf Club on the shores of the Moray Firth. The Old Course is essentially the hallowed grounds of the golf world. It's the oldest and arguably most iconic golf course in the world, having been founded in the 1400s. Nairn, developed in 1887, is basically like a brand-new course in the grand scheme of Scottish golf.

We played the Old Course first, and I opted not to hire a caddie. Now, much has been written about the famous St. Andrews caddies, and I can tell you that the ones I met were fantastic. But I didn't want to hire one, so I didn't. Although it was raining and windy, I still managed to play a fairly decent round of golf (my actual score is not important). I hit the ball well, never got too lost, and managed to have a lovely day.

I woke up the next day fully prepared to repeat the previous day's excellence. Since I had managed the Old Course without a caddie, I didn't even think about hiring one at Nairn. "Who needs 'em?" I thought. What I didn't know was that Nairn is perhaps a bit more challenging than the Old Course. I went on to have one of the most brutal days of golf I've ever played. The only way to truly enjoy golf is to learn to enjoy it even when you're playing badly. Where did I learn that, you ask? At Nairn, for sure.

Playing the Old Course, I didn't ask for help simply because I didn't want to. And at Nairn, I didn't ask for help because I didn't think I'd need it. Both of these approaches were foolish for different reasons, but at the core of both was a similar problem: passively allowing the status quo to lead me, rather than taking the initiative to learn and then do something.

I'm not the only one who has made this mistake, and I think we can learn a lesson from how others have responded in similar situations. Michael Hyatt is an author and leadership consultant, but he was once the leader of the publishing company Thomas Nelson. He had just transformed his division at Thomas Nelson from an under-performing part of the company into the most profitable. But he realized he had run out of leadership "tricks." So what did he do? If you've been paying attention to anything I've said in this chapter, you probably guessed it—he hired a coach. Hyatt realized he didn't know what to do next, and instead of pretending or coasting off his past accomplishments, he went out and found someone who could help him become a better leader. He even credits his career success to a series of amazing coaches. He avoided my two golfing errors: not doing anything and not knowing when I might need help.

Great leaders are not lazy or passive. They don't accept the status quo or wait for others to come to them. They take initiative, especially in learning where they might need help, where they might need to grow if they want to improve. And that's the difference between good and great. That's the difference between a leader who lets time slide by and one who is oriented to the future, what I call an aspiring leader.

Your Future Self Will Thank You

The truth is that none of us can see the future. We can't know everything that's coming our way. We can make educated guesses, but our perspectives are inherently limited, so preparing for the future is something of a sucker's game. That's especially true if you are doing this on your own. But we can always do better if we have others to help us. There's a reason why creative problem-solving meetings always involve more than one person—extra perspectives help us discover better answers.

And that's why you need a coach, even if you aren't in an official, paid leadership role yet. Not only can a coach help you see solutions you may not have imagined to problems you haven't fully understood, but they will help you learn to ask the right questions, questions that will help you self-evaluate. Self-evaluation and introspective questioning are two keys to becoming the leader you want to be. They can help you prepare for a future you can't see clearly yet.

So much is changing so fast today. We'll always be newbies at something. I often think about this quote by Kevin Kelly from his book *The Inevitable*. It perfectly encapsulates why choosing humility today will help me be a better leader tomorrow:

> Technological life in the future will be a series of endless upgrades. And the rate of graduations is accelerating. Features shift, defaults disappear, menus morph. I'll open up a software package I don't use every day expecting certain choices, and whole menus will have disappeared.
>
> No matter how long you have been using a tool, endless upgrades make you into a newbie—the new user often seen as clueless. In this era of "becoming," everyone becomes a newbie. Worse, we will be newbies forever. *That should keep us humble.*
>
> That bears repeating. All of us—every one of us— will be endless newbies in the future simply trying to keep up. Here's why: First, most of the important technologies that will dominate life 30 years from now

have not yet been invented, so naturally you'll be a newbie to them. Second, because the new technology requires endless upgrades, you will remain in the newbie state. Third, because the cycle of obsolescence is accelerating (the average lifespan of a phone app is a mere 30 days!), you won't have time to master anything before it is displaced, so you will remain in the newbie mode forever. Endless Newbie is the new default for everyone, no matter your age or experience.[2]

Tomorrow's leader understands that they don't—and won't—understand everything. They know they're an endless newbie. They know their weaknesses and strengths, and they are ready for what will come, because they have invited someone into their life to help maintain an awareness of where they need help.

A coach is someone who comes alongside you to help you remember the lessons you've learned. Forgive me as I apply every single sports metaphor in getting this message across. There's a reason coaches spend their first practices working on the basics. These are the foundational practices on which players build their skills and then their (hopefully) winning season. The coach doesn't quit after honing the basics, though. He stays with the team all season—teaching, reminding, encouraging, challenging, and helping the players see whatever they need to see to perform at their highest levels.

A River of Relationships

A good friend of mine, David Wills, explains it in this way. Imagine you're in a canoe going down a river. In this river, you need three groups of people to make this experience the best it can be. First, you need someone downstream—someone who has been here before and can tell you what's coming. Second, you need someone upstream—someone you can pass advice back to who can learn from what you've experienced (think: those you are leading). And third, you need someone in the canoe next to you—someone who can share in the present joys and struggles as they happen.

Poor leaders have people only upstream. They are learning how to manage this river at the same time that they are shouting to the people behind them, giving directions as quickly as they can. Sometimes they get it right, but a lot of times they don't. No one is alongside them when they succeed or when they fail, and the people behind them are often stuck learning how to fend for themselves.

Good leaders have people upstream, and they have people alongside them too. They have friends and peers and coworkers who share in their journey, and they lead moderately well. They're figuring out the flow and curve of the river as it comes to them, but at least they're not experiencing it alone.

Great leaders have all three groups of people. They have upstream folks they are leading, as well as people alongside them. And they have a guide in front who is coaching them, teaching them, instructing them, and helping them prepare for what's ahead. Even better, those who are alongside and behind them glean insights from the same downriver advice. And trust me, those in the canoe behind them couldn't be happier to receive counsel from someone who knows what they're talking about.

Leaders who have no one ahead of them are frequently plagued by fears and doubts, constantly wondering whether they can handle what's next. Or they may feel overwhelmed, having no time to dream about the future because it's coming at them so fast that all they can do is react. What's even worse is that the people they're "leading" are experiencing much of the same.

Great leaders determine what the top priorities are and why those things are at the top. They anticipate the rapids ahead. "Can we do it?" and "How do we do it?" are secondary questions. They first figure out what "it" is, and discovering the answer takes the discernment of a great coach.

For Tiger, his "it" wasn't just winning tournaments. "It" was having a perfect golf swing. Winning was the by-product of improving himself, and that happened only because he asked for help. Butch Harmon knew Tiger's swing could be better, and he knew how to make that happen, freeing Tiger to focus on the "what" and "why" ("I want to have a perfect swing because I want to dominate"). Together, they made history.

The future will be full of leaders who have coaches. Plain and simple. Having a coach or guide or mentor is now a standard prerequisite for achieving your future goals as a leader. No one is asking you to navigate the river of leadership alone. I'm saying the opposite—don't do it alone!

Don't let pride or laziness (or both) keep you from asking for help. Adopt a posture of humility, following in the footsteps of the GOATs who have gone before you. The people you lead don't want to be left out to dry, without clear direction for the future.

They want to follow someone who has been there before. Do you?

CHAPTER 4

Leaders Never Fail— They Just Have Loads of Expensive Learnings

To say Dennis Rodman is eccentric is an understatement, kind of like saying that Elon Musk doesn't stop at gas stations. Off the basketball court, Rodman is known for his motorcycles, his colorful hair, his tattoos and piercings, and his short fling with Madonna. On the court, though, he is considered by many as the greatest rebounding forward of all time.

A full episode of *The Last Dance*, a ten-part documentary chronicling Michael Jordan's 1997–98 Chicago Bulls, was dedicated to understanding Dennis Rodman and the art and science of rebounding. For Rodman, rebounding was way more than luck or even hustle. It was a studied skill for him.

As Rodman explains in the film, he would take friends to empty gyms and have them shoot from all different angles. As the ball caromed off the rim, he would study the position of the shooter, the trajectory of the shot, and the angle of the bounce. But his research and studies went far beyond that. Rodman also learned the tendencies of the shooters he commonly faced: "I'd just sit there and react. I just practiced a lot about the angle of the ball and the trajectory of it. You got a Larry Bird, it's gonna spin. You got a Magic, it'll maybe spin. When Michael shoot over here, I position myself right there. . . . I just start learning how to put myself in a position to get the ball."[1]

Rodman made a career out of understanding and executing remarkable, once-in-a-generation rebounding. In addition to the five titles he won with the Pistons and Bulls, Rodman was enshrined in the Naismith Memorial Basketball Hall of Fame in 2011. For his career, he averaged 13.1 rebounds per game. But Rodman's most astounding statistic is that he finished his career with an NBA-record 159 games with twenty-plus rebounds. No one else has more than ninety-five.

Simply put, Dennis Rodman understands rebounding. He planned and prepared to take a miss and make something from it. And becoming a rebounding machine is the leadership of the future.

No Regrets, All Rebounds

In this new dawn of leadership, you and I must learn how to rebound. A rebound is simply recapturing the ball after you've missed a shot. And you will miss. Rebounding *assumes* there will be missed shots. And the put-back scores just as many points as if the original shot were made. Sometimes the rebound even leads you to an easier shot.

For aspiring leaders, learning to rebound from a missed shot is vitally important because *when we know there is always the potential to rebound, we are less likely to be afraid to shoot.* Fear of shooting the ball—making a big decision, taking a risk—can paralyze many leaders. Great leaders are not afraid to shoot, even when they know they may miss. One reason is that they've learned to rebound.

You might be tempted to put this book down right now, thinking, "I've heard this before: be willing to fail faster to find success sooner. Been there, done that, and I turned in the Uber receipt for it."

But hang with me. That's not where I'm going.

Remember, the world is changing. Rapidly. The sooner you learn this, the better off you'll be. After all, the world is not slowing down. Why should you?

Trust me, if you believe that being a great leader is about win after win after win, you'll miss out on so much. Your ability to adapt to the future of leadership is contingent on your ability to grow comfortable with failing. Becoming a great leader is about being willing to take risks and being adept at learning from your failures without getting lost in them.

And beware: *not* learning from your mistakes is the quickest and easiest way to become a failure. The good news is that doesn't have to happen to you.

To be remarkable at anything, you have to be *more willing to risk failure* than anyone around you. Accept that failure is frequently a prerequisite to success. There *will* be missed shots, so you must learn how to rebound from them.

You don't have to dye your hair pink or become infatuated with Madonna, but if you want to become the leader the future is demanding, Rodman should be your guy.

The Hierarchy of Fear

Have you ever wondered why we're so afraid of failure? Me too. Let's dig into that.

Obviously, all fear that we feel is real, but not all fears affect us the same way. If we were to line up all the types of fear and have a competition of which lingers longest and affects us most, one kind of fear would stand on the top podium and receive a gold medal. And others that are just less powerful. Knowing that there are varying degrees of fear doesn't change our circumstances—we still feel fear—but it can help to strip some of the power from that fear. This fear hierarchy (see diagram) has helped me to contextualize my fears. The higher the fear is in this hierarchy, the more power it has over me.

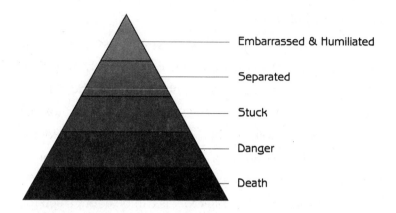

Embarrassed & Humiliated

Separated

Stuck

Danger

Death

Danger and Death

On the bottom row we have the loss of life, a fear of *death*. All people have some fear of death, but it may surprise you to hear that there are stronger fears. I saw a refrigerator magnet that says: "I am not afraid of death. I just don't want to be there when it happens." There's a reason this is true.

Ask anyone with a fear of heights or a fear of flying about why that fear is so strong. They'll tell you it has more to do with safety than it does with dying. That's why feeling *danger*, or a loss of safety, is a rung higher than death itself. Fearing the loss of safety also explains why many people are afraid of spiders and snakes. People don't fear those creatures merely because they're creepy; people fear them because of the harm they can cause. Death is scary, but for most people the feeling of danger is even worse.

Separated and Stuck

Continuing up the pyramid, we have the loss of freedom. Consider this: Do you know anyone who always takes their own car or feels a strong need to be in the driver's seat whenever the team goes to lunch? They fear a loss of freedom or autonomy. That feeling of losing your freedom, of not being in control, of being *stuck*, is real to a lot of people. Movie theaters, churches, sporting events, or any other environment with big crowds can be a tough sell for someone with this fear. They desperately cling to a need for control, and they hate anything that might limit them from moving ahead.

Just above the loss of freedom is the loss of relationship, which is synonymous with a fear of being *separated*. Many men and women are walking around with scars of rejection from their pasts. This fear doesn't leave us. It lingers. And if it's not dealt with, it affects every relationship we'll ever be in for the rest of our lives. Even now you might be remembering a relationship that left you feeling rejected.

Did you ever get that eerie feeling that comes just before a breakup? It's both a gift and a curse from our soul, alerting us that something is about to go down. I felt that way as I sat in my parents' white Volvo 240 DL with Rachel, a girl I had been dating. I had sensed the impending conversation for a while. I'd hoped that dinner at Chili's and then seeing *Men in Black* together would turn things around, but Will and Tommy Lee let me down that night.

"So what do you think about us going out again?" I courageously and awkwardly asked just before she slipped out of the car into her parents' house. Little did I know, the only open door was the one I gave her to drop this line on me.

"I just don't think God wants us to date."

Oh, you have got to be kidding me. You're playing the God card on me? Fortunately, I'm a pastor now, and I can laugh about it, but what she told me that night was not only that she wasn't a big fan of mine but that God evidently wasn't either. That's dating rejection with a side of divine rejection as well. Clearly, I'm not over it . . .

The need for acceptance is baked into us like cheese baked into macaroni. It explains why conflict or the giving of critical feedback is so difficult. We want to be accepted more than almost anything. And when rejection happens, people often do one of two things to make sure it doesn't happen again:

1. They run right into another relationship, hoping to find that acceptance they're looking for.
2. Or they close themselves off relationally, making it difficult for anyone to get back into that part of their soul again.

When these tendencies show up in leadership, the consequences are brutal for all who follow. Leaders who run recklessly from risk to risk, desperate for a win, and leaders who avoid risk altogether, never chancing a loss, are both ineffective.

Embarrassed and Humiliated

Jerry Seinfeld's joke about what people fear is one of the best: "According to most studies, people's number one fear is public speaking. Number two is death. Death is number two. Does that sound right? This means to the average person, if you go to a funeral, you're better off in the casket than doing the eulogy."[2]

I don't know if Jerry is familiar with the hierarchy of fear, but he certainly understands that the fear of potential humiliation is stronger than the fear of death itself. That's why the fear of failure—a fear that who we are and what we do will be rejected—lands at the top of the fear hierarchy. Many of us have tied what we do—our performance—to who we are. And when we fail in life, we begin to see ourselves as failures. And that's probably one of the most difficult things we can experience.

Failure challenges the most sensitive aspects of our personhood. It disturbs the ego and leaves us feeling embarrassed, ashamed, and humiliated. And the worst kind of failure is the kind that happens in front of others. It's why if you were to ask me about my most embarrassing moments, I'd tell you these stories:

- When I was in tenth grade, I was the emcee for the Miss Central High School pageant. I was so excited to play such a prominent role that I passed out in the middle of the event, right there on the stage. And, no, it wasn't during the swimsuit competition.

- In high school I finally saw my name in the lineup at shortstop for our varsity baseball team. When I tried to backhand the first ground ball hit to me, it took an odd bounce, hit my wrist, rolled up my arm, ricocheted off my chin, and mysteriously went down my shirt . . . without my knowing it. I was running around, feeling like an idiot, when the coach finally yelled, "It's in your shirt, *moron!*" (I may have added that last word, but that's what I heard.)

- I once spoke in front of a group of college students with the front zipper of my pants down. That's right. A forty-five-minute talk. I didn't realize it until one of the students texted me about it on the way home.

The feeling of embarrassment is paralyzing. Who knows how many great ideas it has stifled? Who knows how many moments of bravery or courage it has shut down? It can certainly keep you from stepping out and risking your self-esteem. Remember the No Fear brand from the 1990s? Well, you can slap those stickers all over your life, but it's not enough to conquer the feeling of failure.

I'm afraid to fail because it would be embarrassing.

I'm afraid to fail because I believe others would hold it against me.

Worse, I'm afraid to fail because I worry that people will label me a failure.

When we wrongly associate who we are with what we do, as if that is the most important thing about us, our performance in life will inevitably control us. And when we make mistakes, we will interpret those mistakes as judgments against us.

But here is the truth: you'll never make the basket if you never take the shot. And you'll never shoot if you're afraid to miss. So how do you get past your fears? Accept that you *will* miss. Plan for it. More often than not, it's the miss that leads to the make.

Burn the Lasagna

In the first few years of our marriage, Jenny and I met with a counselor. In several of our sessions, he was digging into our reluctance to take risks and said, "You know what you need to do? Invite some guests over for dinner and then burn the lasagna. I mean, just scorch it. Leave it in the oven so long that it smokes. Then tell them you're sorry, order pizza, and see what happens. You'll get over it, they'll get over it, and it'll become a story you laugh about."

Yeah, right. Way easier said than done.

But stop and think about that advice for a moment. What was this counselor saying to us? He wasn't suggesting that failure is always easy (it isn't). He wasn't saying that failure won't have consequences (it will). No, he was saying that as difficult as failing might be, we need to learn to be comfortable with it. And that is possible. In fact, it's something I'm currently learning.

Becoming comfortable with failure has been the toughest part of leadership for me. It's definitely not something I've mastered, but I'm growing more and more comfortable with my failure. One reason is that I've had more failures in the past few years than I had in my entire life before that. My confidence in myself and in my ability to always land successfully has taken some hits. I feel like a two-week-old Georgia peach—a little sensitive and slightly bruised.

I didn't plan to fail. Aside from our counselor's bizarre advice, I had never even thought about *planning* to fail. Usually I've stepped out with an idea, requested a budget for it, rallied staff and volunteers together, and then poured loads of time, energy, and heart into the work—only to see it shut down because my bosses deemed it a failure. That's when failure hurts the most—when you've put your heart and soul into a project.

I've spent loads of mental energy trying to diagnose the reasons for my failures. Why did it happen? What could we have done differently? Was something from the plan? Was it the execution of the plan? The truth is that sometimes projects, ministries, and start-ups don't work. We all know that. And the reasons are plentiful.

- It may have been too early; the world wasn't ready for it.
- The resources ran out before enough momentum could build.
- The leader of the project wasn't the right person to pull it off.
- There were too many products similar to it, and the competition was too stiff.

Whatever the reason for the failure, it was painful—and still is. It may have been embarrassing, in some cases even humiliating. My failures affect me at a deep level. They have left me gun-shy and risk-averse, often questioning my own abilities.

But what's the other option? Not to risk? Not to try? To play it safe? To plan and plan and plan until you know beyond a shadow of a doubt that it'll work? Well, that's impossible. The only upside to my season of failures is that I am now somewhat of an expert in recovering from failure. Remember, no idea has a guarantee of 100 percent success. Learn from the failure? Yes. Dwell on the failure? No. At some point, you have to push your chips in and take a risk. You will never make the shot you never take.

And how do you recover from failure? It's a bit like bouncing back from a sprained ankle. You give it time to rest. You grieve the sprain. And you grow from what you learned so you don't make the same mistake again.

Give It Time

If I had to use a word to describe my life right now, I'd say *hurried*. Everything is quick, rushed, and hustled. Spend one morning with us trying to get our kids on the school bus on time and you'll understand what I mean. Perhaps your life feels like that as well.

When you experience the pain of failure, it can be tempting to rush past it, pretend it didn't happen, look for simplistic excuses, or try to ignore it. But you'll never learn from your mistake if you don't slow down and do the difficult work of taking a closer look. Give it time. But don't waste that time. Consider your life prior to the failure. Talk to others involved. Debrief and try to avoid casting blame, looking instead for lessons to learn from the failure.

That failure is just a speed bump on your journey. Slow down enough that you don't scrape the bottom of your car, but don't let it stop you. If you rush beyond the failure, you'll miss the opportunity to learn. Sometimes you just need a breather because it took so much out of you. Don't become obsessed with the what-ifs of how you could have done it differently. Take some time to rest, relax, and rejuvenate. Treat yourself with some love and care without jumping right back on the horse again.

Grieve the Sprain

Unfortunately, many people walk around in life with a limp because they never recovered from a failure in their past. Maybe the failed project still affects their confidence, they still blame their boss for being passed over, or they've never recovered from having to apologize onstage for the misguided joke at the recent leadership conference they hosted. (If that last point was oddly specific, it might be because I was making a note to bring up that experience with my counselor at my next appointment.)

Have you seen the tragic experience when one failure leads to another failure? We all know two failures don't necessarily make a success.

A failure always involves some kind of loss, and losses need to be grieved. The good news at this step of recovery is that you don't even have to admit you failed in order to see your need to grieve. Whether it was truly a failure or not, grieving what you lost is always healthy. Why? Because failing to grieve means nurturing the pain, and bruised egos almost always buckle under the pressure of future risk. Do yourself a favor and work through the denial, the anger, the bargaining, the depression. Eventually you'll reach a point where you've accepted the failure and are ready to move on to the next risk.

Grow from What You Learned

There is a difference between a growth mindset, which says that I can always improve and I can always grow, and a fixed mindset, which says that the skills and knowledge I have are what I have—no matter what I do, it's not going to change. In her book *Mindset*, Carol Dweck lays out the danger of getting stuck in a fixed mindset. On the negative side, too many people with a fixed mindset take on the role of the victim by telling themselves, "I can't take a chance because I don't have what it takes." They let doubt and fear control their future. But the other side of a fixed mindset can be equally dangerous. Some fixed-mindset people don't learn from their mistakes and are unrealistically positive, always believing deeply in their own abilities and giftedness. They have a superior view of self and are blind to their weaknesses. Here's how Dweck puts it: "Fixed-mindset leaders, like fixed-mindset people in general, live in a world where some people are superior and some are inferior. They must repeatedly affirm that they are superior, and the company is simply a platform for this."[3]

The alternative to a fixed mindset is a more flexible growth mindset, believing that all of life is a laboratory. Successes do not mean we've arrived. Failures do not mean we're doomed. All life's experiences, whether good or bad, are opportunities to learn from and grow through. This mindset better enables us to face the unpredictability of the future.

We make a failure pay up by squeezing every ounce of learning out of it. Rebound from this missed shot, and you will overcome your fear, ready to put up the next shot.

Fighting the Fear of Failure with Actual Failure

Let's try something. Have you taken any risks lately? Tried anything that hasn't worked out as you'd hoped? Can you name a failure you've had in the last year? The last month? This week?

If not, you need to develop a plan to succeed at failing. Because failing is the best thing to break the power of the fear of failure. The very thing we need to do to face our fear is the very thing we're afraid of doing. Clearly, that's not easy, but learning to fail successfully can happen only by failing. You can't learn it by reading a book or watching someone else do it. You have to take the risk, fail, and learn how to work through it. And if you plan to fail, starting by taking small risks and progressing to larger decisions, you'll probably find out that you'll be okay. You'll live to see another day.

I want to encourage you to try two strategies for failure: fail small and fail forward.

Fail Small

When I was learning to communicate from a stage, the best advice I received was to say yes to every opportunity that came my way. Nothing beats experience. Doing something over and over again is a great teacher. And in those early days of learning how to speak in public, the stakes were much lower than they are today because the stages and the crowds were much smaller.

At this point in my career, any ease or comfort I feel in speaking on a stage before thousands of people is largely due to all the failures I experienced early in my career. I'm sure there will be additional failures down the road, but learning to fail early on, in smaller settings, helped me overcome those initial jitters, worries, and doubts with relatively minor consequences.

The business equivalent to a small crowd is something author and researcher Alberto Savoia refers to as a "pretotype"—something between an abstract idea and a prototype.[4] Savoia's work with Stanford University, Google, and many other Fortune 500 companies has led him to discover that *failing fast through the earliest stages of development of what you're hoping for* is the most cost-effective way to determine whether a product has potential.

North Point Ministries has repeatedly reaped the benefits of utilizing these smaller models of experimentation to the point that the phrase *pretotype it* has become common language for us. For example, instead of overhauling our new guest experience, we tried a simpler process to connect new guests who attended Easter services. We were able to learn from it on a small scale before rolling it out as a more permanent solution. The pretotype gave us a sense of whether it would work on a larger scale.

Fail Forward

Again, remember that the key to failure is learning from it. Failing small—taking risks in small ways so the consequences are less severe—is one way to learn. Realizing there are no wasted failures is not just spinning the failure into a positive. No, it's better than that. It's learning to grow, progress, and evolve in ways that otherwise wouldn't have happened. I call this failing forward.

A few years ago, we created a new kind of service for emerging adults. Even though we didn't intend it to be, it became somewhat of a public project because of the attention it garnered. We ended up fielding loads of calls, emails, and messages about it from other churches. I was even asked to speak at a few conferences on why we were starting it and how we were thinking about it. Ultimately, the service ran for two solid years before we determined that it wasn't taking off like we wanted it to. And so we shut it down.

The courage it took for me to roll out something new surprised me. And because it took so much courage, when we shut it down, I felt like such a failure. I blamed myself, believing if I had led it better, it would have worked better.

After all was said and done, what we learned from this service was tremendous. It changed the way we saw the future of our church. We engaged with hundreds of people who are still involved in our church. Our team learned to innovate in ways that we wouldn't have otherwise. We learned many lessons from the project, but the temptation to feel like a failure was still pressing.

After much soul-searching, I had to decide that the benefits were worth the risk. I had to learn from the experience and not be labeled by it. I had to allow the failure to propel us forward.

This is what I lean on most in my own personal faith.

Too many people claim (wrongly) a dangerous promise that Jesus never made. They believe Jesus said that by following him we would avoid pain and suffering. Nope, quite the opposite. (See John 16:33 to see the actual promise.) Jesus never promised us a pain-free life, but he did tell us that he would make our pain *matter*. And that promise is powerful, helping us to embrace the pain and failure in our lives. If we learn to see the redeeming value in our pain, we will be further equipped to fight the fear of failing again. Our perspective shifts, and we can see the misses of life as teachers and not as irrevocable judgments on our worth and value. We resist seeing failure as something that labels us and steals our identity.

An easy way to apply this idea is to keep a running list of your failures, noting not only the failure itself but also the learnings that came from that failure. This simple habit forces you to reflect on the failure and acknowledge the lessons learned. As you celebrate what came about as a result of the failure, you'll find yourself failing forward—looking toward the future with hope and anticipation—instead of allowing past failures to knock you back.

The Starting Line Is Painted with Failure

The most important company ever to come out of Silicon Valley is one you've probably never heard of. The founders of General Magic set out to change the world. They had a vison for a small device that closely resembled the smartphone sitting near you right now. But the world wasn't ready for what they created, and eventually General Magic was buried and forgotten. The company was a failure.

But many of their ideas and talented people moved on, finding their way to companies such as Apple, Microsoft, Motorola, and Sony. The tell-all, inspirational documentary on this monumental project claims, "So much that came out of General Magic is the foundation of everything we take for granted today."[5] Little did the founders know that when the company went out of business—a failed venture at the time—they were not facing the end of the road. They were staring at the beginning of something new. And that's how aspiring leaders need to think about their failures—both the ones they have made and the ones yet to come.

> Failure doesn't have to be the end.
> Failure can lead to a new beginning.

This statement is more than a bumper-sticker, feel-good message to tell yourself when you're sad. I'll say it as plainly as I can: *being unafraid of failure is an essential quality of future leadership.* The sooner you grow comfortable with your potential for failure, the sooner you'll be ready to face the reality of our ever-changing future.

I don't want you to come away thinking that failure is fun. Failure never feels good. Over the last few years, I've had plenty of opportunities to learn from the pain of failure, and quite honestly, my confidence has been shaken. I've had numerous conversations with my bosses where we had to walk back through a project I led, because it ultimately was deemed a failure. Thinking about it still hurts, even years later.

Tomorrow's leaders cannot be paralyzed or tormented by failure. We have to think differently. We have to see the risk of failure not as something to avoid on our way to the finish line but as its own starting line for whatever race we hope to run.

CHAPTER 5

Be Aware of Your Weaknesses but Intimate with Your Strengths

In 2004 a part of me thought I would one day look like Brad Pitt in the movie *Troy*. I thought—or at least dreamed—that a perfectly chiseled set of washboard abs was within reach and that a girl would soon follow.

Unfortunately, the washboard-abs dream never became a reality. But I did end up getting the girl, which I guess means that of all the characters in the movie *Troy*, the one I most resemble is . . . Paris?

If you're unfamiliar with the movie (and you really should watch it; it's a fantastic flick), you should know that being compared to Paris is not ideal. He's the guy who steals another man's wife, starts a massive war, and then chickens out when it's his turn to fight in it. But Paris's real flaw—his Achilles' heel, if you will (sorry not sorry)—is his lack of self-awareness.

Paris has little awareness of his strengths and weaknesses. We see this play out in the movie when he challenges Menelaus (whose wife Paris stole) to one-on-one combat even though (a) Paris is a terrible hand-to-hand fighter and (b) their duel could never stop the inevitable war that has emerged at the gates of his city. When Paris didn't understand his own strengths, he succumbed to his weaknesses.

Paris's brother Hector, on the other hand, is a master of self-awareness. Hector knows his strengths so well that he uses them to cover his weaknesses. He's a great fighter, yes, but he leans heavily on tactics, wit, and self-control, which he knows his enemies lack. With Achilles out of the battle, Hector routs the Greek army day after day simply by playing to his own strengths. In Hector, we see a masterful war technician—and also a self-aware prince.

Hector is the best fighter the city of Troy has to offer, yet even he knows he is no match for Achilles. Hector knows his strengths so well that he also knows their limitations. So what does he do? He keeps the battle for Troy focused on the city's impenetrable walls, where his strength and the strength of the entire city lie.

Now, as for how that story ends, I'll have to let you watch it for yourself (spoiler alert: it has something to do with a horse that isn't what it seems). But what we can take away from the characters of Paris and Hector is how important it is for a leader to be self-aware.

Self-awareness is the foundation on which every virtue is built. Virtue (and, as I'm about to argue, leadership) stems from a twofold understanding of who you are and who you are called to be. It's about knowing your strengths and using that understanding to develop those strengths into a legitimate superpower. Socrates said, "To know thyself is the beginning of wisdom." But he gave us only half the picture. The other half comes from Proverbs 9:10: "The fear of the LORD is the beginning of wisdom."

If you want to become the best leader you can be—if you want to be the person God created you to be—start by knowing yourself and then let that knowledge shape how you treat others and how you see God. This self-awareness includes knowing where you are strong (what you do well) and where you are weak (what you are not so good at). When you know your weaknesses and when you're intimate with your strengths, you can use the latter to cover the former. But even more, when you know your weaknesses, you can turn them *into* your greatest strengths.

Strengths or Weaknesses?

There's a reason these are the two most commonly asked interview questions:

"What are your greatest strengths?"
"What do you consider to be your weaknesses?"

Both questions make sense. Having been on both sides of job interviews, I know why someone would want to know the strengths and weaknesses of a potential hire. One reason we ask this is to get a sense of how well people know themselves, and knowing your weaknesses is a good gauge of self-awareness.

Of course, by now everyone has a scripted answer to this interview question, making it essentially useless. "What are my greatest weaknesses, you ask? I care too much. I work too hard. I expect too much of the people around me." Cool. Me too. You're hired.

If you were to answer both of those questions for real, though, what would you say? This isn't an interview, so you can be honest with yourself. Are you more intimate with your strengths or with your weaknesses?

Many people find it easier to see their weaknesses. One reason is that we tend to view our weaknesses as changeable and our strengths as permanent. A 2016 study showed that people perceive their weaknesses as more malleable than their strengths.[1] The people in the study reported that they expected their present strengths to remain constant, but they expected their present weaknesses to improve over time.

This is understandable, as most of us want to think we will get better at things we aren't good at and retain the strengths we already have. But we see an odd phenomenon when we couple that expectation with the fact that *almost every other study about weaknesses and strengths says we should focus on improving our strengths rather than fixing our weaknesses.*[2] When we focus on our strengths, we are happier, experience less stress, feel healthier, have more energy, feel more satisfied with our lives, are more confident, experience faster growth and development, are more creative and agile at work, experience more meaning in our work, and are more engaged in our work. To top off all that, leaders who focus on the strengths of those around them experience improved team performance and greater success.

Know Your Weaknesses

Why, then, do we spend so much time camped out on our weaknesses? We have this strange bias about ourselves in that we think we will naturally improve on our weaknesses, but we take our strengths for granted.

It's normal to spend more of our energy thinking about situations that went wrong. Have you ever left a party where you had a great time, but then spent the entire drive home thinking about the one tiny moment when you put your foot in your mouth and said or did something awkward? We always remember our failures. We never forget what didn't go well.

Weaknesses are like blind spots in a car. Everyone has them, and we have to figure out how to live with them. Many newer car models now have cameras and warning lights to help us manage our blind spots, and that's great. But whenever you're merging lanes, you should still look over your shoulder and make sure no one is in your blind spot.

Your personal weaknesses are much like this. You should always seek to be aware of the times, situations, and circumstances in life and in your leadership style that might lead you to struggle, fail, or compromise. But don't spend days and weeks and months camped out on those issues, working to improve or resolve them. Instead, acknowledge that they're there and come up with a system that helps you thrive despite them.

In a recent interview, Grammy Award–winning rapper Lecrae was talking about starting his label, Reach Records. In discussing the entrepreneurial journey, he said, "I love staffing my weaknesses."[3]

Staffing your weaknesses.

Lecrae is known for his thoughtful commentary on culture and society and where the future is headed. With that simple comment, he can now add "leadership genius" to his résumé. What he was saying was that he recognized there were areas of the job he wasn't equipped to excel at. But instead of working hard to improve his abilities in those areas, he hired people who were already good at doing those tasks.

It's startlingly obvious and simple, isn't it? You can do the same thing. Of course, we may not all have a personal assistant or coworker who can make up for our weaknesses. But we can surround ourselves with people who know us intimately and who can help us at least see, if not fix, our weaknesses we tend to overlook. Similar to the importance of having a coach, we are often most effective when we see ourselves as part of a larger team, a community where various gifts and abilities work together toward a common goal.

Be Intimate with Your Strengths

Let's go back to the movie *Troy* for a second. Paris knew his weaknesses. He knew he wasn't a good fighter; he knew he wasn't particularly big or strong. He was certainly no match for the massive king and warrior Menelaus. Yet knowing his weaknesses didn't set Paris up for success. He didn't put his knowledge to good use.

Hector, on the other hand, knew his strengths and never exceeded their limits. He knew exactly how far his archers could shoot from their walls. He had a literal line in the sand that he wouldn't take his army past. Instead, they stayed within the range of their archers and let their enemies come to them. Being intimate with his strengths meant Hector knew the limitations of his strengths—and he embraced their limits. The minute you don't know the limitations of one of your strengths, it flips from a strength to a weakness.

Imagine I'm a deep-sea fishing expert. I have a fleet of boats I use to take people out to sea. I have helped people catch all types of fish, I've never been seasick or scared of the sea, and let's be honest, I'm a great time. Let's say you came to me wanting to go on a deep-sea fishing expedition. You and I are out on the boat. I'm showing you around, pointing out some of the best spots and introducing you to the equipment we'll use. Now I take you over to your fishing rod, and I talk about how the fishing line used in this rod is the best of the best. It's an unbreakable line woven together with thousands of millions of microfibers that are military-grade strength (whatever that means). You can reel in anything.

What if I gave you this incredible sales pitch right before you found out that the fishing line is only seven feet long? You could drop it only a few feet off the side of the boat and that's it. Not only is that fishing rod useless to you, but all the incredible characteristics I just shared with you are moot. Despite all the strengths of this fishing line, the limit to how far it can go out to sea makes all the difference in its usefulness. Being intimate with your strengths means not only being aware of what you're good at but also knowing the natural limitations that come with each strength.

Today we have several different personality tests that measure our strengths, but we often stop digging into our strengths after receiving the results. You may learn, for example, that you're a good communicator. If that's your strength, wonderful. But what type of communication are you particularly good at? Writing? Public speaking? And what is it that makes you a good communicator? Is it a skill you understand well enough that you could teach it to someone else? Those are the one-level-deeper questions we need to ask to become *intimate* with our strengths.

Here we take the opposite approach to knowing our weaknesses. You want to know and acknowledge your weaknesses, but you don't need to explore every nook and cranny in that house. But for strengths, you do, because these are the characteristics you will lean on if you want to be a great leader. Know your weaknesses, but be intimate with your strengths. You have to know your strengths inside and out, backward and forward, in snow and in sunshine.

One of the reasons many people, perhaps Christians especially, are hesitant to know and understand their strengths is because it feels prideful. Studying your strengths can feel like an exercise in self-congratulation, as if you're constantly patting yourself on the back for how good you are. But studying your strengths is really the opposite of a prideful pat on the back. It takes humility to acknowledge that your strengths have *limits*. Knowing what you're good at isn't enough. You need to understand that you, like every other human being on earth, are good at some things, but even you have limitations.

And finding your limitations is what leads to empathy.

Self-Aware Leadership

The pressure of leadership often brings an expectation of being someone who can do it all. But being the relational police, the problem-solver, the idea generator, and the go-getter isn't really possible for any one person. Those roles imply shouldering more burden than you're capable of bearing. When you're familiar with your weaknesses and intimate with your strengths, you're capable of shouldering the burdens that fit you instead of whichever ones come your way.

Here's the truth: Bad leaders walk into a room preparing to solve whatever problem they're presented with. But great leaders walk into a room preparing to help only in the areas where their strengths match the needs. And when great leaders find problems that don't match their strengths or, in fact, line up with a weakness, they don't bear down and power through. No, they look around at others in the room and find the person who is a better fit for the problem.

Both strengths and weaknesses should remind us of our need for each other.

A few years ago my counselor suggested I read *Leading with a Limp* by Dan Allender. My guess is that this counselor had listened to me gloss over my mistakes, share the most edited version of my story, and give only the details that showed me in the best light. Instead of challenging me directly, he said, "You should read this book." It was delicate, kind, and effective. If this particular chapter is challenging for you, I'd recommend you read it as well.

As you can tell by the title, the book is about leading

with your weaknesses, not in spite of them. When you choose to do so, Allender argues, that will lead to your leadership success and the satisfaction of your people. "To the degree you attempt to hide or dissemble your weaknesses, the more you will need to control those you lead, the more insecure you will become, and the more rigidity you will impose—prompting the ultimate departure of your best people."[4]

So why will the strongest leaders in the future be those who lead with weaknesses? Because your best leadership will happen only when you are willing to be exposed, to lean into your weaknesses so that you can respond, adjust, and grow. Leaders who don't fear transparency and vulnerability earn trust and inspire greatness in others. Being a leader unafraid to show your failures and weaknesses gives others the freedom and permission to take risks and become better versions of themselves.

Of course, there is a difference between leaning into our weaknesses and dwelling on them. We shouldn't dwell on those weaknesses to the point where we can see nothing else, just as we shouldn't ignore our strengths in an attitude of faux humility. Both of these responses sell ourselves short and cause us to fail the people around us. Rather, we should be honest about our weaknesses while exercising our strengths.

When we acknowledge our weaknesses, we acknowledge our humanity. We also make ourselves leaders people *want* to follow. Here's why:

- **Sharing our weaknesses is an exercise in humility and authenticity.** When we hide our weaknesses from others, we shut off a part of ourselves, and that part may be what connects us to someone else. The leaders who work hard to maintain an appearance of "all strength, no weakness" are the ones no one can relate to. Those people don't even appear human. Why would we want to follow them? The best leaders are the ones who ask for help. The best leaders are the ones who know they can't do everything alone.

- **Sharing our weaknesses is an invitation to work together.** When I admit my weakness to you, that's an open invitation to help me, to be better together. The leader who never asks for help is difficult to relate to. Who wants to work for and with someone who never seems to need help with anything?

When we're honest about our weaknesses, we build up our empathy muscles. When we recognize that we're not talented in a certain area, we can better appreciate those who are, *and* we can better relate to those who share our weaknesses.

No one should manage their weaknesses alone. You need the support of others. In the same vein, no one should study their strengths alone. You need the sobering humility of having someone there with you.

Moving beyond Self-Awareness

If you want to be self-aware just so you can better know and understand your strengths and weaknesses, then you're missing the point. The practice of growing in self-awareness is a chance to find out the ways in which you can help those around you.

I once had a seminary professor say that your spiritual gift is whatever you give to others. For those not familiar with the idea of spiritual gifts, they're those things God has instilled in us—the gifts and strengths and talents we possess. My professor's point was that *these are useful only to the extent to which they are used for other people.* Your strengths and weaknesses aren't yours at all, as something to own and possess. Instead, they're gifts given to help you rely on and help others. That's how the body of Christ works.

By being intimate with your strengths, you'll know the best ways you can serve the people around you. You'll know the felt needs you can fill, as well as the ones you can't. And when you come across needs you can't fill, you'll realize you need to know the strengths and weaknesses of those around you so that they can help in the areas where you're not as well equipped. That's when self-awareness leads to others-awareness—when knowing the strengths and weaknesses of others allows you to depend on them for help.

See how the journey toward self-awareness ends up being about other people? That's the final destination. It's not ultimately about knowing yourself perfectly. It's about better understanding each person's strengths and weaknesses and how you can use them to the group's advantage.

Your strengths aren't yours to keep. Your weaknesses aren't yours alone to bear. The more intimately you understand your strengths, the more well equipped you are to serve others. And the quicker you are to acknowledge your weaknesses, the easier it is to ask for help.

Self-awareness works only when it leads you to be aware of other people. You can't be self-aware without also being others-aware, because the minute you stop paying attention to the people around you is the minute you lose self-awareness.

Level up your self-awareness to the point where it improves your awareness of others. That's the mark of a great leader.

CHAPTER 6

Get the Right People on the Bus . . . and a Few Who Aren't So Right

Jim Collins's *Good to Great* is heralded as one of the greatest leadership books ever written. And rightly so. It has sold over three million copies and is praised for its data-driven look at what has allowed the most successful companies in the world to sustain long-term success. Seriously, it's in the Hall of Fame of leadership books because it is three hundred pages of hypotheses, research, analytics, and advice. It's one of the leadership books I refer back to as a textbook when I feel stuck or uninspired as a leader.

Collins's work has been a playbook for hiring and managing teams for a few decades now. I've used his three practical disciplines for making rigorous personal decisions with my younger managers for years.

1. When in doubt, don't hire—just keep looking.
2. If it's obvious a change in personnel is needed, act quickly.
3. Put the best people on the biggest opportunities, not the biggest problems.[1]

These techniques are terrific. This advice holds water for today and will for tomorrow as well.

The phrase Jim Collins is perhaps best known for is one I've had ringing in the back of my head for years now. Every time the responsibility of managing a new team of people comes my way, I try to do what Collins instructs: "Get the right people on the bus!"

Great leaders, Collins argues, don't set a direction of mission and vision and then move full-throttle in that direction without first determining the players on the team. Great leaders focus first on the bus: who shouldn't be on the bus, who should be on the bus, and where each person should sit. As Collins explains, "First Who . . . Then What. We expected that good-to-great leaders would begin by setting a new vision and strategy. We found instead that they first got the right people on the bus, the wrong people off the bus, and the right people in the right seats—and *then* they figured out where to drive it. The old adage 'People are your most important asset' turns out to be wrong. People are not your most important asset. The *right* people are."[2]

"Get the right people on the bus!"

What a phrase. It's simple, memorable, and instructive. You don't even need to have read Collins's book to know what it means: Patiently hire great people. Relentlessly evaluate the ones you already have. Astutely move each person into the right seat. Unapologetically fire the ones who don't fit.

Easy enough, right?

The issue is that after years of trying to build teams with this mantra in the back of my mind, I've come to profoundly disagree with Collins's "get the right people on the bus" message because leading a team into the future requires far more than just evaluating talent for the sake of hiring and firing.

I'm ready to get off the bus.

The Danger of the Bus

Everything should be as simple
as it can be but not simpler.

This quote, attributed to Albert Einstein, speaks both to the value of simplicity and the danger of making something *too* simple. Building a great team is far more complicated than a seating chart on a yellow cheese wagon, and I'm convinced Collins would agree.

When oversimplified, "get the right people on the bus" may lead you to dismiss some people too quickly. You may also miss some opportunities for growth as a leader. You can develop a thriving team by fostering a culture of trust, establishing a clear pathway of development and growth, and facilitating countless small decisions of mutual submission between you as the leader and those on your team.

As we've seen already, great leaders don't go it alone. They understand the value of working with a team that complements their strengths and offsets their weaknesses. You don't need to be convinced of the power of teams. We've all seen the great accomplishments that can be achieved when the right people come together. Steve Jobs once famously noted that the first ten hires at a start-up will determine whether the company succeeds. You need A+ players if you want A+ results. These are the team-mates who produce twice the output of B or C players. A+ players, Jobs learned, run circles around players with lesser talents.[3]

But who are those A+ players? And what does the best team look like? The answer to that question is constantly changing, and it depends on who you are as a leader and what you hope to accomplish. One thing I know is that future teams will be different, far different from what we see today. Much of "getting the right people on the bus" will depend on a leader's ability to assess the talent, resilience, and chemistry of their players *in light of what will be demanded of them.* So aspiring future leaders will need to know how to pull together a great team—how to get the *right* people on the bus, sure—but they will also need to know how to define what "right" even means and what to do when the team inevitably looks different than they imagined.

Let's spend some time unpacking this often over-simplified concept.

Who Are the "Right" People?

One of my coworkers constantly reminds me that we rise and fall based on our definitions. So I want to start by taking a look at that phrase—the *right people.* What do we mean when we say we want the "right" people and not the "wrong" people on our teams? Too many leaders, myself included, have made the mistake of dismissing the "wrong" people.

Ask ten people who they think are the right people for a team or a task, you'll probably get ten different answers. Determining the right and wrong people brings up memories of grade school and categorizing people into groups, keeping certain people in some groups and others out. Clearly we're not just talking about empty phrases like "he comes from money," "she has a cool factor," or "they know other right people." When I think about it, I wonder if I'm even one of the right people.

On the flip side, the term *wrong people* conjures up

negative connotations—words like *challenging*, *toxic*, *complicated*, *pushy*, *ambitious*, and *quirky* come to mind. Depending on what your team is trying to accomplish, you may need some people with these qualities. In other cases, people like this will destroy a team.

Too often individuals have been classified as the wrong person for the wrong reasons—they're different, they're too driven, they're difficult to manage. If you want to be a leader of the future, keep these next three points in mind.

1. Different Is Not Wrong

Being different from others, or a minority within a larger majority, is never wrong. And not only is different *not* wrong, cultivating "different" will be an essential leadership skill for future leaders. Aspiring leaders will need to envision future teams filled with an array of skin colors, class diversity, and various life experiences. Diversity is already recognized as a valuable asset for organizations today; in the future it will be a baseline requirement for success. To understand why that's so, we'll take a seat on an actual bus, on which one moment sparked a tectonic shift toward a more diverse and equitable world.

On December 1, 1955, an altercation took place on a crowded bus in Montgomery, Alabama. Every seat was filled, and that became a problem when a white man stepped onto the bus. As was custom in the Deep South at that time, when a person with white skin needed a seat, the bus driver would ask people with darker skin to give up their seats. In this case, when the bus driver, James Blake, asked the first row of the "colored section" in the back of the bus to stand and give up their seats for the white man, three of the four individuals obliged. One of the four, Ms. Rosa Parks, declined. Firmly planted in her seat, Rosa Parks "sat" her ground.

It was the 1950s, and the American economy was booming, with employees working long hours each day. After a full day of work as a seamstress at the Montgomery Fair department store, Ms. Rosa Parks had tired hands and tired feet. But as she later stated, her fatigue wasn't only from the work she had done that day—it was a different kind of fatigue. "People always say that I didn't give up my seat because I was tired," wrote Parks in her autobiography, "but that isn't true. I was not tired physically . . . No, the only tired I was, was tired of giving in."[4]

The resilience Ms. Parks displayed didn't go unnoticed. Her brave refusal to give up her bus seat is credited as one of the crucial and inciting incidents that furthered the movement of civil rights in America. The world was paying attention then, and it is paying attention now. The ripples of her courage are still felt over six decades later, evidenced by the rising value of diversity, equity, and inclusion in our society and, more specifically, in the workplace.

And here is where we come back to our discussion of the "bus." As the workforce is changing, there is a growing need for teams that value differences, incorporating diverse voices into discussions and decision-making. In the past, diversity, equity, and inclusion were "nice to have." In the future, these qualities will increasingly be "permission to play" values for organizations, churches, and companies. When we see a team where everyone looks the same, an alarm should go off and we'll think, "Oh no. Something's wrong here."

Here are a few perspective-shifting questions you can ask yourself:

- When I look at our team, do we all look the same?
- Am I inclined to read capabilities and potential into people who look like me?
- When I look around our team or company and can't find a lot of different voices or perspectives, could that be a subconscious way I've found to validate myself and my own perspective? How so?
- Are there other areas of my life in which my own perspective alone has been particularly limiting? (Example: seeing life through the eyes of my wife has shown me so much more than I would've seen through my own.)

Getting the right people on the bus is critical to long-term success. But beware that your understanding of "right" doesn't unintentionally come to mean "same." We are all predisposed to give the benefit of the doubt to people who look like us, and knowing that about our-selves is a necessary first step toward creating teams that will be competitive in the future.

2. Driven Is Not Wrong

Many leaders feel threatened by people working for them who are overly ambitious. Ambition threatens authority, and in some cases, a teammate with a drive to achieve may have an off-putting way about them that communicates a focus on personal achievement and raises questions about their commitment to the team. When leaders see this drive, a common response, whether from the boss or from others on the team, is to label that person. And that label can be difficult to remove.

When I find myself threatened by someone's ambition, the problem is typically with me, not with that person. As the Arbinger Institute explains in *Leadership and Self-Deception*, the greater problem is that I can't see that I'm the problem. When I label someone as "too driven," I begin looking for behaviors that justify my accusation. And when I find that evidence, "it's my proof that others are as blameworthy as I've claimed them to be—and that I'm as innocent as I claim *myself* to be. The behavior I complain about is the very behavior that justifies me."[5]

Team cultures that fail to make room for ambitious people will eventually be filled with people afraid of fail-ure. Ambition is a drive to advance, a willingness to take risks, and an openness to failure. Ambition is a powerful value that every team needs to be successful. And those you recruit to your team can't just have opinions about the work they do, they also need to own the results of that work. Appropriately channeled ambition is needed at every level of a growing and thriving organization. It helps teams set appropriate goals, aim for higher results, and pursue those lid-breaking ideas. Mislabeling someone with ambition and drive as the "wrong" person for your team will limit your team's potential to succeed.

3. Difficult to Manage Is Not Always Wrong

There are plenty of senseless reasons we might label someone as "difficult to lead."

Maybe she has some quirks.

Maybe he always wants to do it his way.

Maybe he's trying to drink half his weight in water and often leaves meetings because of the water intake. (Guilty.)

We shouldn't pay too much attention to those issues, even when they seem like glaring problems. Still, it's so easy to let little irksome habits become excuses for writing someone off or choosing not to hire them. But what would've happened to the world if that's the approach Nick Fury took?

When he brought the Avengers together, he did so knowing there were a lot of conflicting personalities, all with their own tendencies and quirks. Tony Stark has a penchant for coming up with nicknames that mock those around him. Thor constantly talks down to people. Captain America is optimistic to the point where it borders on obnoxious. If you watch the Marvel movies, you can clearly see how these personalities clash and how they create both the conflict that drives the plot and the humor that adds to the entertainment value.

To say that Nick Fury "managed" the Avengers may be overstating his role, but at the very least, he brought some big personalities into one room, and instead of combusting (though they certainly came close), at the end of the day, they found a way to work together.

Just because someone's personality doesn't match your leadership style, or just because they don't have the same sense of humor as everyone else, doesn't mean they don't belong. It doesn't mean they're wrong for the bus.

Why Wrong People Can Be So Right

I've never led a team with all the "right" people.

From the middle of the sea of cubicles where I work, I've seen those labeled as the "wrong" people make a world of difference. Every team I've been on, and every team I've led, has had at least one person, and sometimes even a few, who has seemed like the wrong person. Be careful about labeling some people "right" or "wrong," because often the wrong people can help you in significant ways.

"Wrong" People Can Be Most Helpful in Making Right Decisions

I'm a "grip it and rip it" kind of decision-maker. Step out of the cart, grab a club, see ball, hit ball. I know it's not right, and it's gotten me into some trouble. People who read manuals, follow instructions to a T, and reread emails drive me nuts. So it's tempting for me to mislabel people like this as the "wrong" people. But surrounding myself with people who read labels, think things through, and call a few people to verify the details before making a decision has helped me immensely.

The sixteenth president of the United States uniquely understood the value of the wrong people. Instead of surrounding himself with "yes people," Abraham Lincoln did the exact opposite. When constructing his cabinet, he chose political rivals who were likely to disagree with him and challenge him. Imagine the headlines this would make for a president in our day and age of echo chambers and filter bubbles.

> On a blank card, he [Lincoln] wrote the names of the seven men he wanted. At the center of his list stood his chief rivals for the nomination—Seward, Chase, and Bates. . . . While several months would pass before the cabinet was assembled, subjecting Lincoln to intense pressure from all sides, he resolved that day to surround himself with the strongest men from every faction of

the new Republican Party—former Whigs, Free-Soilers, and antislavery Democrats.[6]

Lincoln's decision to diversify his cabinet didn't necessarily make his life easier, but it allowed him to run his decisions through a filter. This paid dividends in his efforts to unify a fractured country and especially in his decision of when to release the Emancipation Proclamation.

By midsummer 1862, Lincoln knew he wanted to emancipate enslaved individuals. It needed to be done, and he forcefully told his cabinet what he wanted. Yet when the issue of timing was raised, Seward saw the situation much differently than Lincoln. Seward wanted the proclamation to succeed, but because the war was going so badly for the North, Seward insisted they wait until after a victory. He believed this would create an easier path for the proclamation. So Lincoln waited.

After the Battle of Antietam was fought and won by the North, Lincoln had his moment. He announced that on January 1, 1863, "all persons held as slaves . . . shall be then, thenceforward, and forever free."[7]

One of the lessons here is that you can't make the best decisions when every person on the bus looks like you, talks like you, and thinks like you. As leaders looking to the future, we need to question our former labels and seek to surround ourselves with people who may have been previously labeled as the wrong people. Not only will our decision-making improve as a wider array of perspectives is brought to us for consideration, but we'll also begin to think more like those we're trying to lead. Keep that bus colorful, challenging, and appropriately noncompliant.

"Wrong" People Will Make You the Right Leader

A few years ago, I found myself managing an enigma. There was a person on our team whom I couldn't figure out. We didn't have much chemistry, and I couldn't see what value he brought to the team, so I struggled to find the right role for him. Yet the teams he oversaw loved him, and his previous manager had lauded, praised, and promoted him. I was in a pickle, to say the least.

As it turns out, the problem was with me, not with him.

A few months into my new role, I worked with our HR team to find him another opportunity within the organization and mustered up the courage to have the tough conversation. "You can't have this job anymore, but you can have that one," I told him. And when he asked why, I told him that he simply wasn't the right person for the bus I was driving. (No, I didn't use those words, but that was the gist.)

Fast-forward four years, and my job changed yet again. Want to guess who was on the new team I was assigned to manage? Yup. Same guy. Oh boy, here we go again.

The situation still perplexed me. I couldn't figure out the value he brought, but the team he managed loved him. So this time I took a different approach. Instead of blaming him, I looked in the mirror. Here are a few things I learned about myself:

- He and I have different communication styles. He's like Flo's Filet from LongHorn Steakhouse: solid steak, nice cut of meat, very little fat, and a good portion of words for one person. Me? I'm more like a thirty-ounce rib eye: great for a celebration, definitely consisting of some extra fat, and probably enough words for two people.
- He puts his head down and gets stuff done. I'm always looking around to see who wants to join up for a group project.
- He uses a more diplomatic and indirect approach to conflict. I'd rather all parties involved in the conflict sit around together, express every thought we've ever had, kiss and make up, and then hold hands while singing "Kumbaya."

The more I thought about my strained relationship with him, the more I realized most of it was on me. My beef with him was really something in me that needed to change. And that's not uncommon in workplace or organizational relationships. When we bump into someone we have a tough time enjoying, it's often God's way of pointing out something in us that needs to change. And so I did.

I began to take a different approach in my interactions

with him. I showed more curiosity about who he was, asked him what he felt he brought to the table, and sought to understand why he was wired the way he was. I was more direct in my questions about his job description and responsibilities. To say everything changed would be a bit of an overstatement, but a lot did change. And we ended up having four successful years working together.

A person I once considered unfit for the bus I was driving became a catalyst for my own personal growth. That's often true with the "wrong" people. They may be exactly the person you need to help you change and grow as a leader. So be careful about writing them off too quickly. Next time you bump into one, take a quick look in the mirror first to see if something in *you* needs to change.

"Wrong" People Help You See the Right Way

Everyone sees the world through their own lens. And we all have different lenses. If you ignore the vast array of perspectives available when you gather input from a diverse team, you end up with monovision. You begin to think everyone else thinks just like you. News flash: They don't.

Whether you hope to lead an increasingly diverse and changing society of people, create an organization to meet a specific need, or build a business around a product that people want, how you *see* will affect everything you *do*. And one of the best ways to expand your vision (and see the future more clearly) is to *have some people on the bus who see the world differently from the way you see it.*

Bringing in different people doesn't have to be purely altruistic either. It's a great way to get better results. It's a great way to be a better leader.

According to the experts at People Management, "Researchers found that when diverse teams (of three or more people) made a business decision, they outperformed individual decision-makers up to 87 percent of the time. Diverse teams were also shown to make decisions faster than individual workers and benefited from a 60 percent improvement on decision-making."[8]

Time to Move On

If, after all we've talked about, you still have reservations about someone on the bus, ask yourself a few questions:

- If the person resigned, would you secretly be excited?
- If you had it to do over again, would you rehire this person?
- If the person were a free agent, would they be hired on another team within your organization?

If the answers to these questions are obvious, don't be afraid to set that person free. Chances are that if this person is in the wrong seat, they'll find a more comfortable seat on a different bus anyway. And if I've seen it once, I've seen it twelve times: someone gets let go from one job, and a year later they see it as the greatest break because of the new opportunity they eventually landed. Careers are rarely linear, and as we look back, we can often see how God uses the twists and turns in the road to put us into the best spot possible.

Being Wrong about the Right Person

One of the greatest experiences you'll have as a manager is watching people grow and change to become better leaders. Learning how to develop people into a better version of themselves is what leadership is all about. There will always be the temptation to believe the narrative you've built in your mind about certain people, but that doesn't mean it's true.

In his book *The Black Swan*, Nassim Taleb calls this temptation "narrative fallacy." Too often we think back on events with error or misinterpretation. Taleb says this should be called fraud, but to be more polite, he calls it fallacy. He explains narrative fallacy as "the fallacy . . . associated with our vulnerability to over-interpretation and our predilection for compact stories over raw truths. It severely distorts our mental representation of the world; it is particularly acute when it comes to the rare event."[9] In the stories we tell ourselves about the past—the people we used to live with, work with, or had the most conflict with—we regularly fall prey to narrative fallacy. It happens with such ease that we hardly even recognize it.

- The "challenging" coworker who used to always talk about himself.
- The "emotionally unhealthy" roommate who never helped clean up the apartment.
- The "insecure" coach who yelled at you to make herself feel better.

The danger of these narrative fallacies, Taleb explains, is that we bind facts together with our own explanations and interpretations, drawing connections that may not exist. I'm certainly not suggesting that you're always wrong, only that sometimes, on occasion, you probably *are* wrong. I'm waving the red flag to help you accept that if you've missed the call on people in the past, there's a chance you'll miss it on people in the future as you're filling out that bus seating chart. We aren't perfect. We all have blind spots and biases.

We all have a proclivity to misjudge people. I hope knowing this will give you a new game plan going forward—an alternative to knee-jerk judgments about who should and should not be on the bus.

Wrong Person or Faulty System?

Before blaming the people on the bus, ask yourself, "Can I lead better? Do I need to lead differently? Or could it be that the system is broken or needs a significant change?" Examine yourself *and* the system you're working within.

The Aspiring Leader's Guide to the Future

The late Dr. W. Edwards Deming, renowned statistician, engineer, management consultant, and author, would argue that the real question we need to ask isn't "Who?" but "What?" In *The System of Profound Knowledge*, Deming explained that 94 percent of variations in workers' job performance levels have nothing to do with the workers themselves. The people are simply not able to outperform the lid of the system, and those same players can find success in *new* systems.[10]

The world of sports has certainly taught us this concept. Some of the most fascinating story lines in the sports world are the worst-to-first championship stories. Think about the 1991 Kirby Puckett–led Minnesota Twins, the 1969 New York Mets with Tom Seaver and Nolan Ryan, or Bill Laimbeer's 2003 Detroit Shock team in the WNBA. The surprising fact behind these rise-to-glory stories is that the nucleus of the team didn't always turn over for their improbable championship run. On the contrary, in most cases the roster of the worst team was remarkably similar to that of the team that finished first.

Too often the problem with the poor-performing team wasn't just the players. Many factors come together for a team's success, apart from those who make up the team. The temptation for every manager, both new and old, is to place all the blame on the players. In doing so, managers are inclined to misdiagnose the past and future, mislabel the bus riders, and undervalue certain members of the team.

A New Mantra

Though it's not as catchy as Jim Collins's bus principle, this is the mantra future leaders should live by:

> Don't dismiss too early. Don't develop too late.
> And lead the ones you have until
> you just can't anymore.

Jim and I agree that getting it right with the people on your team is essential, and getting it wrong is far too costly. Remember, these are *people* we're leading. People with lives and families and hearts and souls and futures. Let's commit to treating the bus roster with as much care and thoughtfulness as possible. That's the way of aspiring future leaders.

CHAPTER 7

You Have to Give
Trust to Be Trusted

When I first learned there was a way to enhance chocolate, my mind was blown. Not quite like the moment I realized Ryan Gosling played a significant role in *Remember the Titans*, but close. (Who knew the guy had so much agility as an actor?)

When I heard the bold claim that chocolate could be enhanced, my first thought was, "Who in their right mind thinks chocolate needs to be enhanced? The center-cut filet mignon of dessert ingredients needs no enhancement."

My second thought was, "Okay, I'll take a short walk down this road evidently lined with funhouse mirrors. *If* it can actually be enhanced, what kind of person has the audacity to think they could do such a thing?"

Then I tried it. And it worked. So excuse me for being hyperbolic, but I feel like it's that important.

Adding a small amount of coffee to any
chocolate dessert changes everything.
And, yes, I do mean everything.

All exaggeration aside (and honestly, I'm not exaggerating), when I find out that something small can make a significant change for the better, I get excited. In this chapter, I want to talk about an ingredient of future leadership that has that kind of potential—something basic and frequently overlooked that makes every relationship and every work culture better. And it's quite possibly the most important ingredient for successful future leadership.

Again, I'm not exaggerating.

That ingredient is *trust*.

Trust: The Currency of Future Relationships

If the devastating pandemic of 2020 taught leaders anything, it's that *in leadership, nothing matters more than trust*. Within a matter of days, every organization had to go all in on a work-from-home model, and that took a measure of faith that the employees were going to do the job they were hired to do without someone standing over their shoulders. Crisis has a way of revealing just how much or how little trust exists in a work culture and in our relationships.

In a matter of days, the rhythms of communication in our relationships changed. Methods of workplace

accountability were disrupted. The cadence of encouragement and inspiration from bosses to employees was rattled.
The well-developed safety net of feedback loops designed
to keep tabs on what was and wasn't working needed to be
retooled. No longer could the boss walk down the hallway
to find out who was in the office and who wasn't. Even
George Costanza's brilliant method of leaving his office
light on, his jacket on his office chair, and his car parked
in his assigned parking spot was now obsolete.

Though our world was already moving toward a get-
your-job-done-at-your-pace, in-your-own-place kind of
work culture, the 2020 pandemic accelerated these trends.
It was as if a decade of change was compressed into
a few short months. As my friend Frank Blake told our
leadership team, "Crises have a way of violently breaking
old habits and starting new ones." And our workplaces,
workflows, and work cultures were thrown into complete
disarray while new ones were formed in their places.

When employees are asked what they want most, all
signs point to a job that includes a great deal of trust. If
you enjoy a data-driven voice of truth, here's a sampling
of the collective and quantitative opinions I'm referring to:

- More than 80 percent of US employees would choose
  a job that offered a flexible work schedule over one
  that didn't.[1]
- As for after the pandemic, 65 percent of respondents
  reported wanting to stay full-time remote employees,

and 31 percent wanted a hybrid work environment. That's 96 percent who desire some form of remote work.[2]

- Just under 70 percent of employees said "not being trusted to do their job" would be *the* leading cause for leaving their job.[3]

Trust has always been a cornerstone of healthy relationships, and it's increasingly important in a future where teams may not work together in the same physical space. If flexibility, freedom, and autonomy are the primary motivational drivers of the future, you will serve yourself and those around you well by becoming an expert on developing and maintaining trust in your relationships. Flip it upside down, inside out, and all the way around so you can learn everything you can about this virtue. Master the art of fostering trust in your relationships and you'll be able to lead in any situation, team, or organization in the future.

Give a Little Rope

Why trust? Trust will be a required element of every relationship and will be needed in every direction of your organizational chart:

- The manager will be required to trust her employee.
- The employee will need a greater sense of trust with his boss.

- Teammates will desire more trust with one another.
- The employee will even need to trust the company at large.

My own initial understanding of the value of trust was similar to my discovery that certain guys on our high school football team were taking creatine to enhance muscle growth: "Ohhh! That's why they're getting so yoked so fast." Teams and relationships built on trust are noticeably different in how they operate and what they can achieve.

A relationship devoid of trust is like a phone with no service; without it, all you can do is play games. Relationships lacking trust naturally drift toward suspicion, skepticism, and cynicism. When we find our company, organization, church, family, or relationship low on trust, the alarms start blaring because we know relationships are on the brink of breaking down.

In *Smart Money, Smart Kids*, Rachel Cruze offers a fabulous illustration involving a rope, relationships, and trust. Rachel's parents, Sharon and Dave Ramsey, used a rope to signify the amount of trust they currently felt in their relationship with each child, with their child at one end of the rope and the Ramsey parents holding the other end. When their kids were honest, responsible, and competent, they were given more rope. When they didn't do the right thing, the parents pulled the rope back in.

When Denise, the oldest Ramsey child, went off to college, her parents celebrated the occasion by giving her a gift. Before she opened the gift, Dave told her, "Denise, we trust you. You make great decisions. You're going to be 250 miles away, and that means we can't hold the other end of the rope anymore."[4]

Opening the gift, she found a rope. Her parents were giving it to her as a statement of their faith and trust in her to make her own decisions.

This illustration teaches us something important:

Trust cannot be demanded or required.

Trust works counterintuitively. You don't get more of it by demanding more of it, requiring more of it, or even asking for more of it. No, it works the other way around. With trust, you foster trust by giving more trust, not less.

Granted, yes, there are times when you need to rein that trust back in—when it has been broken, for example. We'll discuss that later, but first I want you to see that you start by giving away some rope. When you give trust to those you lead, you receive trust in return. It's the principle of reciprocation. If you want it, you first must give it.

You have to give trust to be trusted.

In healthy relationships, the more you trust others, the more trustworthy they become. The less you trust them, the less likely that person will trust you. Suspicion is a self-fulfilling prophecy. And forcing people to earn the rope of trust doesn't work either. Trust works a bit like our judicial system. The system works when we give people the benefit of the doubt. The line at the starting block is "innocent until proven guilty." Relationships work better when we give people that benefit, whether it's with coworkers, friends, family members, or significant others.

Closing the Gap

The choice to trust happens between the ears of the leader. As you'll see in the following graphic, the battleground of trust lies between every action someone takes and every thought you make. As we observe others' behavior, we interpret their actions and make decisions based on our thinking. And in that gap between their behavior and our thinking, we have a choice to make. Our interpretation of the behavior we perceive will determine the level of trust in the relationship.

A positive interpretation widens the gap.

A negative interpretation closes the gap.

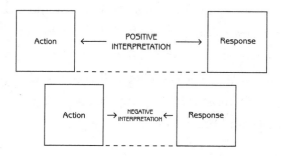

In the heat of the moment, our thoughts and feelings don't seem like choices or decisions we make. Rather, they feel instinctual. And the gap between someone's actions and our response feels minuscule.

We see the event.

We receive the text.

We hear the words coming out of the person's mouth.

And—*wham!*—just like that, the feeling fills us and we respond accordingly. At that moment, we need to force ourselves to slow down and pay attention. That's half the battle. That's why understanding that there is a gap is so important. Before we decide how to interpret that behavior, that event, and even the motive behind the action, we have to force time to slow down. We have to remember a significant word: *pause*. We have to train ourselves to pause and *choose* how we will respond.

Pause.

Choose.

Ask yourself a question: What is the most generous interpretation I can provide for this person's behavior that will lead me to trust more?

Training the mind to pause and choose the most generous interpretation is a mark of a great leader. On the contrary, regularly choosing an interpretation of cynicism, doubt, skepticism, or disbelief will soil any relationship. And as with most decisions we make regularly, there's good news and bad news . . .

- The good news? You can choose to respond to other people's actions with trust.

- The bad news? It takes more than intention. Simply wanting to respond with trust isn't enough. You have to train your mind, which takes diligence, practice, and correction, because trusting others does not always come easily.

A classic example of this is when I receive the following text from my boss:

> Hey Clay, will you give me a call later today?
> There's something we need to discuss.

Truth be told, I felt a twinge of anxiety just writing that. Unless you're one of those unicorns who immediately thinks, "Oh, wow, another promotion?" I'm sure you can relate to the anxiety a text like this produces.

However, it is possible to rewire your brain to inject a sizable portion of trust into the gap between the text and the feeling it produces. Learning to trust that your boss wants what's best, will treat you fairly, and is working toward solving problems for all—whether those things are true or not—fosters the kind of relationship you both want.

Love Making Its Way to Work

Choosing this kind of mental response takes practice because trust doesn't come naturally to us. Out of a need for self-preservation, we instinctively protect ourselves.

The Aspiring Leader's Guide to the Future

A few years back, I was invited to speak to a group of employees at the Federal Reserve Bank of Atlanta. Embarrassingly, I didn't know much of anything about this stellar institution that regulates banks, monitors inflation, and sets monetary policy. What I quickly learned was that they're not in a joking mood down there at the Fed.

When I pulled up to the first of three imposing gates, I said to the guard, "Good morning. I'm here to pick up some bags of cash." That joke went over like a three-hundred-pound pole vaulter.

I'm not sure why I expected security similar to our local Wells Fargo, but I was shocked at how tight they keep it at the Fed and how seriously they take everything they do. I endured a thirty-minute screening process in which I was interrogated, patted down, background-checked, detected for any metal, and repeatedly questioned as to the purpose of my visit. I've never been to Fort Knox, but I can't imagine their security being any tighter than the Fed's. And as we learned from the Bluth family in *Arrested Development*, "there is always money in the banana stand." Evidently there's quite a bit in the Federal Reserve Bank. Like billions of dollars' worth.

I distinctly remember standing in front of the employees and talking about the value of loving and trusting their teammates, when one of their bright finance-trained employees raised his hand to ask this loaded question: "With all due respect, sir, do you realize this is the Federal

Reserve Bank? We don't really talk much about loving and trusting each other. We're taught *not* to trust others."

That gentleman is not alone in his understanding. And you don't have to work at the Fed to think that way. Trusting others does not come easily, and it's not always encouraged in the workplace. Many people and organizations are focused on self-preservation, hardwired to respond instinctually with fear, suspicion, and distrust because it's a cutthroat, dog-eat-dog world. Not trusting is what keeps us alive. Our protective biological response is to put up our fists to fight or put on our shoes to run. Leaning into and leading with trust is far from second nature.

After years of marriage and counseling, I've learned that much of our ability to trust depends on the stability of our childhood. Your family of origin and the events in your childhood can make you susceptible to naivete or cynicism. Some of us have a more difficult time trusting than others. But whatever your past, the future of leadership is going to be built on trust. And you can't change this fact: you foster more trust only when you give it. Future leaders will need to do whatever it takes to build that muscle.

Thanks to my friends at the Federal Reserve Bank, I'm aware that talking about loving others doesn't really fly in a work context. It's too squishy and soft. But forgive me for a moment because I can't talk about trust without also talking about love. Trust and love are like cousins, and you can't have a significant relationship with one without meeting the other. In one of the most profound pieces of literature ever produced, the apostle Paul makes an enduring connection between love and trust. You've probably heard this passage read at a wedding before, but do yourself a favor and read these words slowly: "Love is patient, love is kind. It does not envy, it does not boast, it is not proud. It does not dishonor others, it is not self-seeking, it is not easily angered, it keeps no record of wrongs. Love does not delight in evil but rejoices with the truth. It always protects, *always trusts*, always hopes, always perseveres" (1 Corinthians 13:4–7, emphasis added).

This ancient literature is more than wishful poetry. It's a playbook for healthy relationships. It's a call to an others-first way of life that creates life-giving relationships. Let me rephrase the middle section of Paul's words for the sake of our discussion:

> The best relationships are those where each person works to *protect* the other person rather than protecting self.
>
> The best relationships are those where each person *seeks to trust and trust and trust* until it's hurtful to trust any longer.
>
> The best relationships *hope for change and hope for good*, even when it hurts to hope.
>
> The best relationships *stick it out* when it's tough, *stay longer* when it's hard, and *persevere* in the face of conflict.

Building a work or family culture on the aspirational values of 1 Corinthians 13 is far from easy, but experiencing it is profoundly powerful. In a world where our next-generation leaders often seem more concerned about what works for them than what is actually true and good, these words in 1 Corinthians 13 are the ones that need to be elevated and embraced.

As much as I long for a trust-filled team, it's hard to imagine a culture at home or in the workplace where this is even possible. But just as I've tasted coffee's miraculous ability to enhance chocolate, I have tasted the effects of trust in relationships. At times, I've sensed it long enough to know it is both possible and worth working toward. But it won't happen *without* work and intentionality. It starts when you, as a leader, go first. You can't demand trust or dictate it; you lead by giving it.

Putting Trust into Practice

I can guess what you're thinking: "This idea of leading with trust is lofty, overly optimistic, and other worldly. We live in the real world, and leaders like this are naive." But I am convinced it's possible. Why? Well, what's the alternative? That's not a world I want my children to live in. Even if I'm wrong (and I don't think I am), I'm either bold enough or dumb enough to pursue a trust-filled workplace because I think it's worth it.

In practice, though, I want to give you some pointers

that will help you build this type of culture. My boots are on the ground as I'm trying this every day. And my hope is that the future will be filled with cultures of trust. Here are a few tasks we can start doing today to make this ideal a reality.

Determine How Much Trust Is in the Tank

The easiest place to start is by evaluating your current relationships and rating them on a trust scale. You can't get to where you want to go until you know where you are.

On a scale of one to ten, with ten being the most trust you can imagine, how much trust is currently in the relationship? You might be tempted to just think about this and move on, but force yourself to write it down. After writing down a number, ask yourself, "What would raise that number?"

One of my coworkers, Beau Johnson, courageously asked me in a one-on-one meeting, "I want as much trust as possible in our relationship. How much do you trust me, and what would cause you to trust me more?"

I was caught so off guard, I fumbled through my answer. But after thinking about it for a few weeks, I was able to give him a more thoughtful response and was prompted to ask the same question of him. The honesty and candor of the conversation have made a remarkable difference in our relationship.

It sounds ludicrous, I know. But I encourage you to

walk through this exercise after you've taken the time to assess your own relationships on the trust scale.

Clean the Slate

Most of us have probably been in a relationship where we broke the trust. We shared secretive information with someone else, we showed up late a few too many times, we lost our temper and said something we regretted, or maybe we even lied about something to protect our reputation. One of the reasons I can't imagine living or leading without faith in Jesus is because of the forgiveness he offers. New mercy, endless grace, and full forgiveness are the greatest gifts imaginable. Of course, the consequences of our actions remain, but the fresh start he provides each day does more for my mental health than just about anything else.

And we need to offer that same gift to others. There are a few memorable moments in my professional career when I broke someone's trust, asked for forgiveness, was given that gift, and then was never reminded of my mistake by that person again. I get emotional writing about those times now.

Offering forgiveness is most difficult when the person hasn't recognized the weight of their offense or won't admit to doing wrong. Difficult, but not impossible. I'd encourage you to clean the slate even when the person doesn't recognize that the slate is damaged. In doing so, you give them a blessing they never realized they needed and you accept an apology you may never receive. In some broken relationships, this might be the only path forward.

Ask for Clarity When You Feel Suspicious

As you've read this chapter, you might have thought, "Well, this seems like a recipe for getting hurt. I've been burned before. Forgiving like this means I'd just be a doormat, getting walked all over time and time again."

You're not wrong. We live in a broken world, and sometimes when trust has been broken, a boundary needs to be put in place. Sometimes maintaining the relationship, even one at work, is irresponsible for your own health. Broken trust heals only through honesty, accountability, and sustained faithfulness.

The best relationships have feedback loops of honesty and authenticity. The best cultures are filled with relationships that aren't devoid of conflict but rather marked by healthy conflict. If your boss hurts your feelings, you should circle back with them to ask for clarity: "When we had that conversation about how I led the meeting, it felt as if you were criticizing my leadership. Just curious, was that the message you meant to send?"

Too often we read between the lines, placing suspicion, cynicism, and distrust in the gap. Imagine how much better every relationship would be if we were able to directly appease any suspicion with an ample amount of truth, honesty, and candor about what was communicated. This kind of approach will become increasingly valuable in a virtual work culture.

Have Imaginary Conversations with Generous Explanations

You and I both have imaginary conversations all the time, especially in moments when we feel hurt or when the trust in a relationship is depleted. My counselor calls this rumination, and the longer I've sat with him, the more I've realized how much ruminating I do, not only on past conversations but on future ones as well.

As easy as it is to let your mind wander to the version of a future conversation that helps you feel better about yourself, the *best* way to learn to give a healthy amount of trust is to have imaginary conversations that are best for the relationship. Let's be honest about this: if you can imagine having a conversation where you spout all your frustrations with the confidence of Jack Welch, the attitude of Kevin Hart, and the sarcasm of David Letterman, then you can also rehearse that conversation with as much generosity as you can muster.

The Future of Innovation Demands Trust

If I've heard it once, I've heard it a thousand times: "Daddy, look what I built!"

Every parent knows what I'm talking about. Kids' desire

to show their parents what they've built, drawn, or created is almost insatiable. Why? Because we want someone to be proud of what we've done; we continually seek affirmation. Specifically, we want our authority figures to approve of our work. And we're devastated when they don't.

So even on my worst days, I try to stop what I'm doing, notice something specific that child has done, and use encouraging language to build them up: "Look at what you've done! You have worked really hard on that. I love how you've colored outside the lines. Don't ever let someone tell you to keep it between the lines. You were made to explore the page. Go where your heart wants. I love it!"

Okay, my response isn't always so flowery, but you get the gist.

I hope the words I use with my kids carry a sense of honesty to the work, encouragement for the heart, and love for the child. Why? Because I want more trust in the relationship. I want my kids to know that when I say, "Well done!" they can trust my word.

Every one of us needs that same trust. Let's be leaders who speak not only words that are true and honest but also words that build trust, because the future depends on it—not only the future generations but also the future workforces, workplaces, and work cultures.

CHAPTER 8

Conflict Never Gets Easy, Goes Away, or Feels Great

Remember the episode of *The Office* where Dwight euthanized Angela's sick cat, Sprinkles, without her permission? Let's talk about that.

If you haven't seen this episode, Angela was in a relationship with her coworker Dwight. When she learned he had "removed" her cat without asking her, she was deeply bothered and broke up with him. Never one to be accused of being emotionally aware, Angela went into a tailspin for the next few episodes. Phyllis, Angela's coparticipant on the party planning committee, felt the brunt of her angst. The relational discord between the two of them offered Phyllis an open door to try out some new conflict resolution skills.

The Aspiring Leader's Guide to the Future

Spoiler alert: It does not go well.

> **Phyllis Lapin:** (*Cuts to confessional.*) Angela is worse than usual lately, and we have a party to throw, so I googled "How to deal with difficult people." And I got all of this. (*She holds up a few sheets of paper with information.*) So we're gonna try out some new things today.
>
> **Phyllis Lapin:** (*Cuts back to the office.*) So how do you feel about the fact that the banner says "Lunch"?
>
> **Angela Martin:** I feel angry. Angry at you. Angry at you for doing something stupid. Angry at me for believing you could do something not stupid.
>
> **Phyllis Lapin:** (*Phyllis looks down at the sheets of paper.*) I'm so sorry to hear that. That must be awful.
>
> **Angela Martin:** It is awful. You've made this day awful.[1]

I'm never sure whether to laugh or cringe when I watch this exchange. But it highlights something worth our attention. You can't ignore the ever-present reality of relational discord. And leaders need to know how to deal with conflict. The ability to address interpersonal conflict is a key leadership skill, and that's not going away anytime soon. If you want a healthy culture at work or at home, you must develop the skills needed for healthy relationships.

That's why the conflict between Angela and Phyllis isn't as funny to me as most scenes from *The Office*. It touches a nerve because their behavior highlights several problems I observe in our society at large.

1. Conflict is everywhere, especially at work.
2. People are less and less equipped to deal with difficult situations.
3. Googling advice on how to handle conflict brings a sense of hope.
4. Despite our best attempts, conflict rarely ends well.

In my line of work, I've been forced to grow comfortable with conflict. I don't *enjoy* it—I'm not some kind of mad masochist. But I've sat down with numerous couples to work through tumultuous marriage challenges, business partners fraught with cheating scandals, parents dealing with their teenagers' drama, and young adults trying to convince a parent to go to rehab. These conversations are the 10 percent of life that consumes 90 percent of our emotional capacity.

Yes, I deal with a lot of conflict through my job. But no one warned me that some of the most challenging conflicts I'd encounter would be in my relationships with coworkers. If you employ people, lead a team, or work with others at any level, you're going to find yourself amid conflict. It's a reality of working with people. In this chapter we'll learn to better understand why conflict happens, hone our skills for dealing with it, and see why this matters for your future as a leader.

Future Conflict

As a society, we're not becoming more resilient. Truthfully, we're growing conflict avoidant and, with each passing day, even less skilled at dealing with the interpersonal challenges of everyday life. The relational discord of childhood is now following us into the workplace. Future leaders will require a well-developed set of conflict resolution skills.

For one, our workforces are engaging in conversations previous generations avoided. This means you'll need to grow comfortable talking about difficult topics that require vulnerability. Difficult conversations—"anything you find it hard to talk about"[2]—are not what they used to be. There was a day when those conversations were simply about asking for a raise, ending a relationship, giving difficult feedback, or saying no to the grocery store clerk soliciting a donation for the latest charitable opportunity. Today the topics cover the spectrum of race, gender, politics, and religion, and they are far less taboo and much more likely to come up in the workplace or around the dining room table with friends and family. And this trend will only become more prevalent.

Social media can be a barometer of the changes we see in emotional intelligence. When social media first began, we saw pictures of family gatherings, pets, and everyday life. And we still see some of that. But now people take to social media with their opinions and complaints about what's wrong with this world and what's wrong with others, and these discussions are not always handled with wisdom and care. Too many of us would rather just post about our bad relationship than deal with it. Every time a breakup happens through a tweet, text, or direct message, I'm sure the executive producers of *The Bachelor* just smile a little bigger, knowing it somehow means more drama for their future seasons.

Another measure of our declining relational competency is the odd phenomenon known as helicopter parents. Those of you born before 1980 have probably noticed how differently you were parented than the generations that came after you. In those years, a parent, usually a mom, would throw open the door and say, "Go play outside and don't come back in until dinner." There were no cell phones, no GPS tracking devices, and no pedometers to measure how far you had wandered from home. Now it seems parents are getting their kids smart phones almost as soon as they walk, just to keep tabs on them.

Julie Lythcott-Haims said she had already noted the consequences of this shift when she stepped down as dean at Stanford in 2012: "I had interacted not only with a tremendous number of parents but with students who seemed increasingly reliant upon their parents in ways that felt, simply, *off*. I began to worry that college 'kids' (as college students had become known) were somehow not quite formed fully as humans. They seemed to be scanning the sidelines for Mom or Dad. Under-constructed. Existentially impotent."[3] That's alarming.

Researcher and author Dr. Tim Elmore cites this parenting fail as one of the most devastating challenges facing the generation of kids and now young adults born after 1990. Because of the technology they were born with and shaped by, Dr. Elmore refers to this generation as Generation iY. Although parents may intend to communicate love and support, "these damaging parenting styles that prevent kids from preparing for the real world"[4] have dealt this generation a difficult hand. "The unfortunate result is that kids get ambushed by adulthood, and they retreat."[5]

In *The Coddling of the American Mind*, Greg Lukianoff and Jonathan Haidt argue that we're witnessing a scary decline in conflict resolution skills, and this is clearly seen in many college students on campuses today. The authors tell story after story of offended, fragile, and triggered students who are incapable of dealing with the challenges of real life. In the same way a body atrophies after spending an extended period of time in bed, when students are given a pass from learning to engage in constructive conflict head-on, they fail to develop the skills of empathy, conversation, compassion, and resolve, and those relational muscles slowly deteriorate.

Lukianoff and Haidt wrote, "What is new today is the premise that students are fragile. Even those who are not fragile themselves often believe that *others* are in danger and therefore need protection. There is no expectation that students will grow stronger from their encounters with speech or texts they label 'triggering.'"[6] Instead of being characterized by head-on engagement with challenging and potentially conflictual conversations, students' future social and relational growth will continue to be stunted and impaired. And we'll likely see more aversion to any kind of relational conflict with a boss or coworker going forward. But it doesn't have to be that way.

A Tempered Approach to Conflict

I want to give you a simple plan for approaching conflict. This plan is future-proof, battle-tested, and one-size-fits-all. It won't solve all your problems, but going into a tense situation with a plan is so much better than not having one. As hopeful as you might be when you begin a difficult conversation, hope alone may not be enough.

The first step is to put in a little preparation. It took me years to realize that preparing for a tough, high-stakes conversation is a game changer. Though it's not a magic bullet, often it's the difference between resolution and regret. Preparation is the one thing Phyllis did right that we can all learn from. Start with some alone time and force yourself to get to the root issue, to develop some questions of curiosity, and to plan your ideal next steps.

This plan includes four simple steps, alliterated to stick in your long-term memory system: (1) affirm, (2) ask, (3) acknowledge, and (4) advise. Don't rush through this section. And make sure you stay until the end, where you'll find a John Grisham–worthy plot twist.

Step 1: Affirm

The first step is crucial because any high-stakes, emotional conversation needs to start with a sense that this is a safe place. Establish boundaries so the person does not feel threatened. Start the difficult conversation by affirming something positive about the person: "Angela, I want to have this conversation with you, but first I want to tell you that I have a lot of respect for you. And I really enjoy working with you."

Obviously, don't say anything untrue, but do force yourself to say something meaningful. Again, this is where preparation comes in handy. Give yourself the freedom to develop these thoughts in advance. If you wait until you're in the heat of the moment, that's tightrope-level danger. You may or may not come up with the right words. So give yourself the safety net of preparation to make sure you say exactly what you want to say.

If you have trouble knowing what to affirm, here's a

little trick. Think about the next tough conversation you know you need to have. What's your greatest fear? That the person will be mad at you? That he will hate you? That her feelings will be hurt?

Then start there. Just affirm the very thing you're afraid of. For example, you could say, "As I've thought about this conversation, I don't want you to think that I'm leaving. Because I am not."

As difficult as the conversation may be, make sure the person knows you're willing to have this discussion because you care about them as a person. Don't make this a compliment sandwich, but make it a meaningful declaration of your best intentions for that person and for your future with them.

Step 2: Ask

Too many people go into difficult conversations thinking they fully understand the situation or have the other person solved like a sudoku puzzle. Missing this step will come back to bite you if you're not methodical, humble, and genuinely curious. Force yourself to sit down with a blank notepad and write out all the questions you could ask about the situation. This will help you establish a posture of humility and create a positive atmosphere for even the most difficult conversations.

"Angela, has anything happened lately that's causing you to carry more stress than normal?"

Asking questions benefits all parties involved. It forces

you to admit that there is much you don't know. It immediately communicates care, concern, and compassion. And it gives the other person the floor to talk and you the opportunity to just listen. There's a good reason the authors of the New Testament recorded Jesus asking over three hundred questions. And you don't have to be a math major to understand the simple logic of my grandmother's advice: God gave you two ears and only one mouth for a reason.

Step 3: Acknowledge

For the last ten years, my wife and I have mentored engaged couples who are interested in being better prepared for marriage. We tackle all the tough topics like intimacy, money, and in-laws. But I have the most fun with the session on learning to communicate with each other, specifically during conflict. We ask the couple to bring up one of their latest and greatest fights, and we walk through it with them. And, yes, it's as bad as it might seem. Although they do leave in a better place, it takes some time to get there. We've had plenty of nights when we thought the couple was going to cancel the wedding as a result of the conversation we had.

In that challenging session, we try to teach them that every moment of communication has two critical roles: the sending of the message and the receiving of the message. When there is a breakdown in the sending or the receiving, there is always—and I mean *always*—miscommunication.

This is why spending time practicing the art of assertive communication and active listening is worth every second. Making your partner read your mind rarely ends well. And thinking you've understood what the other person said when, in fact, you heard something totally different is also problematic.

By the way, every conversation, whether at work or at home, has the potential for misunderstanding. Because of that, learn to state back what the other person has said without agreeing or disagreeing with it, defending yourself, or bringing solutions. After you affirm what you can affirm and ask as many questions as you need to better understand, it's time to state back what you have heard, either with the exact same words or with your own version of what you heard. This is the third step in your plan for conflict resolution. As simple and basic as this seems, it's an immediate feedback loop for you to clarify how much you understand about the situation and how the other person sees it. If you're wrong, the other person will tell you you're wrong, but you won't know until you've acknowledged what you heard.

Step 4: Advise

After the first three steps, then and only then are you ready to advise or give the critical feedback you want to offer. Resist being critical, though. The temptation is to point out everything that's wrong with the other person, with the relationship, or with the organization. Don't take the bait.

Pointing out problems is a pointless power trip.

Naturally, it makes you feel more powerful, but without solutions, your criticism doesn't move anything forward and rarely makes a difference. Instead, seek to offer solutions that can bring change, make something better, or improve the quality of the relationship.

And refuse to let the issue define the relationship between the two of you. Imagine the two of you sitting side by side, working on the problem together. Even if the other person tries to put the conflict between you, don't allow that to happen. Put the problem on the table, and get on the same side of the proverbial booth. Real progress is made when you can work on the problem together. Stay in that posture and the advice you give won't even feel like advice.

The Twist

I promised a plot twist, so here it is. For this method to work, you have to do it in the exact order I gave it to you. If you don't, it will *not* work.

If you try mixing up the order, you'll have to walk back through it all in reverse. If you bang on your boss's office door to *advise* them on some situation, you'll end up having to *acknowledge* you were wrong, *ask* for forgiveness, and *affirm* that you'd prefer to stay employed.

Beginning the conversation by seeking to *affirm* what is true about the other person implicitly creates trust and puts you in a healthy posture for a challenging conversation. Then when you *ask* questions about the situation, you model curiosity and you might even learn something that changes your perspective. When you *acknowledge* what you have just heard, you strengthen the bridge of communication in the relationship. And finally, after you have gone through that process, you are ready to *advise*.

Conflict is never easy, but follow this plan with preparation and intentionality, and you can grow this skill.

Conflict as a Gift

In *The Obstacle Is the Way*, Ryan Holiday flips the perspective on difficult challenges we face, including conflict we have with others. Instead of seeing conflict as what's *in the way*, Holiday encourages us to see it *as the way*. "The obstacle in the path becomes the path. Never forget, within every obstacle is an opportunity to improve our condition."[7]

Too often we see conflict as an impediment to the peace we're seeking rather than seeing it as the path to peace. Think about a common conflict you have right now. What if you chose to view it differently? What if you saw it more as something that could produce change in you rather than in the situation or in the other person? Seeing conflict this way can radically develop the future leader within you.

Leaning into this choice has become one of the ways

God is growing me as a leader. You don't have to see relational conflict through the narrow lens of solving the problem of that relationship. There is more in this for you and me. Learning to better handle conflict makes us better leaders. The work of resolving conflict with others is a crucial part of our own personal growth.

Holiday punctuates this idea by highlighting that the conflict you experience or the obstacle in your path just might be your greatest growth opportunity. The impediment can become the path.

> Great individuals, like great companies, find a way to transform weakness into strength. It's a rather amazing and even touching feat. They took what should have held them back—what in fact might be holding you back right this very second—and used it to move forward.
>
> As it turns out, this is one thing all great men and women of history have in common. Like oxygen to a fire, obstacles became fuel for the blaze that was their ambition. Nothing could stop them, they were (and continue to be) impossible to discourage or contain. Every impediment only served to make the inferno within them burn with greater ferocity.[8]

James, the brother of Jesus, underscores a similar idea in his short but stout letter in the New Testament. He instructs fellow followers of Jesus to view conflict or trials they experience as fuel for growth, not as mere obstacles. He wrote, "Consider it pure joy, my brothers and sisters, whenever you face trials of many kinds, because you know that the testing of your faith produces persever-ance" (James 1:2–3). Note that James doesn't say we have to be grateful for the conflict but that we can see value in what the conflict *produces*. James teaches that conflict has an embedded gift—that pushing through obstacles will eventually lead to a better version of ourselves, or in his words, a more "mature and complete" version (James 1:4).

Practice Doesn't Make Perfect

Conflict isn't going away, and as a leader, you need to realize it's par for the course. Conflict is always around the corner, and it inevitably happens in every leadership role. Those who are waiting and hoping for conflict to disappear, or think it is something you graduate from, are living a pipe dream. It never goes away, no matter how long you've been leading.

My high school baseball coach always used to encour-age the work we did on our fundamentals with this ridiculous phrase: "Practice makes perfect." I can still hear him shouting it from across the infield. He would usually follow it up with another coaching phrase: "Don't do it until you get it right. Do it until you can't get it wrong." I still remember the first time I heard him use that saying. It's simple yet profound, and as someone who enjoys a phrase that pays, I enjoy the word-play. But while these are good motivators for learning to field a ball, they don't work with conflict. Practice is good. But you will never get conflict perfectly right. Something will always go wrong. You will use the wrong tone. You will make a distracting statement that will derail the conversation. You will be too rushed in the process or move too slowly to have the conversation. The longer I've led, the more I've realized I'm never going to be perfect at this. It's inevitable that I'll get it wrong sometimes.

But don't let that stop you. Lean into the conflict for the sake of the other person, for the sake of your own growth and, if nothing else, for the sake of the future leader the world needs you to be. This is one skill I can guarantee you will not regret developing. As with many aspects of leadership, you'll never get it all the way right. Even still, the fight is well worth it. And your ability to navigate the conflict will get better and better with each conversation you have.

CHAPTER 9

The Strongest Leaders Will Lead with Vulnerability

There are two words in the English language that, when paired, have the power to elicit powerful emotions like fear, anxiety, panic, and even mild rectal discomfort. What words, you ask? *Job interview.* My palms are sweaty just writing about it.

Most of the time it doesn't matter what the job is. I felt just as much pressure interviewing for summer jobs in high school as I did for my first "real job" out of college. Job interviews can be the source of an inordinate amount of pressure. If you're early in your career, you might feel like your entire financial future is on the line or that this moment could be the difference between a life of purpose—waking up each day excited to crush your goals—and a day-to-day grind working for "the man." Or this interview might represent a showdown with your ego, deciding whether you have what it takes to live up to expectations.

Job interviews can be pivotal moments in our lives, but they rarely determine our fate in the ways we think they do. And yet they're still nerve-racking. I think much of that is simply due to the social dynamic they create.

When you have a job interview, you feel as though your next big opportunity rests on the approval of an individual or group of people. And if someone's approval stands between you and your dreams, you want to be at your absolute best, right? So what do we do? We work hard to create the perfect image of ourselves. We touch up every flaw. We spice up our résumés. (I've seen interns' résumés that would make the accomplishments of a Harvard-grad Olympic medalist with a Nobel Prize for solving global poverty look positively average by comparison.) We choose the clothes to nail the look. We practice speaking with confidence, like we deserve this job. We talk about our weaknesses in ways that make them sound like strengths. And in every way possible, we polish our images to a fine shimmer.

And that's okay in a job interview. The problem is that for many people, this is how they approach leadership. Every day I see leaders show up like they're interviewing for their jobs. As if every ounce of influence rests on the approval of others. As though any sign of weakness or imperfection will cost them what they've spent their lives building.

I understand why people try to lead this way. It has been a common leadership strategy in past generations: *show the best, hide the rest.* And I'll level with you. In some cases, this is still good advice. It's essential in a job interview. It's great for a first date. (You should probably withhold the fact that you're still on your parents' cell phone plan until at least a few dates in.) And for a long time, this advice worked as a successful leadership strategy.

At certain times and in certain cultures, leadership has been primarily about getting people to accept your authority by paying deference to your position. Taking on a leadership role involved assuming a particular kind of posture in relation to others, a leader-like pose that you held when people were looking. Being a leader was about powering up so that others understood that yours was the most important voice in the room.

As you read this description, you may have been reminded of a leader you've met or known at some point in your life or career. Perhaps, when given the chance to voice an idea you had, you were met with a condescending, "You know, that's actually not a terrible idea." (As if to say, while you might have gotten lucky with this singular half-decent idea, you shouldn't forget your place in the food chain.)

I've heard some leaders meet criticism with, "I'll try being nicer if you'll try being smarter." Ouch! Leaders of the past did love the sick burn.

Or perhaps the best of the bunch is the underhanded

compliment, "I like you. You remind me of me when I was young and stupid."

Probably all of us have been tempted at some point to use these same "power-up" phrases. Why do we do this? Part of it is fear. Fear of being replaced or outshone. Fear that someone will find out we're not who we pretend to be. Part of it is narcissism, which lurks in the shadows of every leader's heart. Part of it is the desire for control. Much of it is insecurity. And sometimes it can be simple pragmatism. Exercising authority from a position of power can deliver immediate results, and truth be told, at least for a short period of time, some people will respond positively to that kind of leadership.

One of my favorite examples of this type of leadership is from Will Ferrell's cameo on *The Office* as Deangelo Vickers. When office manager Michael Scott decides to move to Colorado, he is replaced by Vickers for a short stint. As he undergoes training from Michael, in an effort to win the respect of the office staff and differentiate his leadership style, Deangelo has a barber come to his office to give him a straight-razor shave, with the blinds open for everyone to see. The office bullpen fawns over Deangelo's open display of masculinity. Ryan, the temp, calls it "So hardcore!" and Phyllis describes it as a "real power move." Not to be outdone, Michael has the receptionist run to the store for some shaving foam and a disposable razor and joins Deangelo in his office to undergo what looks to be the razor-burn equivalent of nails on a chalkboard. And unfortunately, parodies are parodies because of how close they hit to reality.

Leadership Power Moves

Power up. Posture. Pose. That has been the currency of leadership for a long time. But as anyone who has done yoga can tell you, any pose becomes impossible when you try to hold it for too long. And today, in our current cultural moment, this style of leadership is dying. Leadership that relies on maintaining superiority over others is unsustainable. Leaders who lead like they're constantly interviewing for the job may never get around to doing the work. And eventually it shows. They lose influence. They bleed trust. And if any of that "power-up leadership" is still alive, we need to take it out back and shoot it, because it will not work in the future.

You don't have to take my word for it. Much smarter and more experienced people have come to the same conclusion about the need for a change in leadership posture. Jim Collins spells it out brilliantly in *Good to Great*. When Collins set out to explore the question of how companies move from being good companies to great companies, he referenced the prevailing wisdom that had suggested the key was in the charismatic personality of an executive leader. Historically, those responsible for hiring chief executives looked for big egos and domineering personalities to lead their organizations. And you can hardly blame them. The most recognizable and celebrated executives up to that point had mostly fit that mold. Think of the stereotypical portrayal of C-suite executives you've seen in most movies and TV shows. Words like *ruthless* and *cutthroat* come to mind.

What Collins discovered, however, was counter-intuitive. The results of his research showed that companies who made the step from good to great were led by "Level 5" leaders. A Level 5 leader is characterized by traits that are rarely combined in a single individual: humility, strong will, intense resolve, and a tendency to give credit to others while assigning blame to themselves. Collins states it this way: "The most powerfully transformative executives possess a paradoxical mixture of personal humility and professional will. They are timid and ferocious. Shy and fearless. They are rare—and unstoppable."[1]

For a long time, leaders were expected to be willful, ferocious, and fearless. Many successful leaders have built careers on those characteristics. But leaders of the future must be willing to hold this drive to succeed in tension with humility and gentleness. This is not an easy tension to manage. Leaders of the future must resist the temptation to choose one over the other. They won't always be required in equal measures in every situation. At times a leader's strength and determination will be required to navigate a storm. At other times, humility and deference will be required to make sure that the best ideas rise to the top regardless of who comes up with them. But all these characteristics are necessary tools in a leader's tool kit. Knowing when to pull out the right one, or when to balance one with another, is the mark of great leadership. It's not easy. Of course it's not. But it's worth striving for because our own lives and all we touch will be better for making the effort.

I think what Jim Collins addresses is an eternal truth about leadership. While it hasn't always been in vogue, humility always has and always will win the day.

The Humble Improve

You might be familiar with the word *humility*, but I want to take a moment to define it for you. Humility is often misunderstood, but humility is the foundation of vulnerability. Too often humility is associated with those who lack drive or ambition. Some confuse humility with a lack of courage or a crushing sense of self-deprecation. If you search for *humility* in a thesaurus, you'll find it associated with words like *sheepishness*, *self-abasement*, *mortification*, *bashfulness*, *passiveness*, and *resignation*. I promise I'm not making this up. Who would want a boss or a president whose leadership style could be described using any of those words? These words are not inspiring. If I'm following someone into battle, I don't want them to be sheepish. I wouldn't even want to hire someone whose decision-making and work ethic were characterized by passiveness. But despite its proximity to these words in a thesaurus, true humility is nothing like this.

Here is a good start: "Humility is not thinking less of

yourself; it is thinking of yourself less."[2] That small statement is a myth buster. Humility doesn't require you to think of yourself as inadequate or of little value. It doesn't mean you lack confidence in your ability to do your job well. It doesn't imply that you underestimate your level of talent or skill. It simply means you don't spend your time obsessing about these things. And leaders who are less self-consumed have more time and attention to make better decisions and focus on the needs of those they lead. Humble leaders are just as talented, smart, and determined as egocentric leaders—but they're more agile. They've given themselves space to adjust to changing circumstances. They improve because they're open to criticism.

Okay, sounds good, you say. Then why isn't every leader humble? Great question. I think it's because humility requires two traits that terrify almost everyone: transparency and vulnerability.

People with power and influence tend to feel threatened by the idea of transparency. There's a reason politicians, celebrities, and wealthy business people are inclined to live in homes surrounded by towering walls and to drive cars with tinted windows. Politicians are notorious for campaigning on calls for greater transparency in government, only to try everything possible to avoid scrutiny once they're elected. It's an age-old cycle. Why? Because those with power and influence have more to lose in allowing people to see beyond the surface.

Transparency doesn't mean you give everyone

permission to pry into your personal life or sift through your credit card statements. It means you allow people to peek behind the curtain to see the influences that shape your leadership and the processes you use to make decisions. Our aversion to transparency lies in the fear that if people knew who we really are, they wouldn't respect us anymore. But unless you are corrupt, malevolent, or incompetent, this simply isn't true. Rather, the opposite is true. Increased transparency increases trust.

This may come as a surprise to you, so make sure you're sitting down for this next sentence.

No one expects perfection from you.

No one.

That might be hard to accept. But allow me to take a weight off your shoulders. Most everyone realizes that we are flawed individuals. People don't expect us to be paragons of human perfection any more than we expect it of them. We hope our bosses will make wise decisions, but we expect them to miss the mark at times. We hope our politicians will be honorable in their dealings, but we understand that sometimes they'll fail. The same goes for you. But you don't have to hide it like it didn't happen.

Owning Your Origin Story

When I was growing up, the *Superman* movies were extremely popular. I remember how handsome and suave Christopher Reeve looked as he traded his specs for a cape and bravely saved the people of Metropolis from harm. But what made Superman so intriguing was his backstory: an orphan from a dying planet, adopted by kind farmers, he discovers his powers by accident but sees his efforts thwarted time and again by his weakness to kryptonite.

The superhero movies that have recently topped the box office charts are popular because the heroes are compelling. And there's a reason why, with every superhero, the writers have taken time to carefully craft and detail their origin stories. Superman's origin story, for instance, helps us understand his motivation, his aims, and his purpose. Without those, he's just a really strong dude in tights, and every LA Fitness in town is already full of those. Without the journey, Clark Kent is interesting but not compelling. What makes these characters so inspiring are their fraught histories, their human frailties, and their triumph over enormous challenges.

Leaders are constantly tempted to edit their stories. Whether we're trying to raise capital, attract donors, inspire action, or cast vision, we tend to sanitize the parts of our stories that don't fit the narrative. We do this because we fear that certain parts of our stories might compromise our credibility. But doing so is a mistake. Leaving out parts of your story will never increase your credibility as a leader. It will only increase your anxiety about your leadership.

Worrying that people might find out what you left out can be far more damaging than allowing people to hear the whole story and judge for themselves. Usually the fact that you trusted them with your whole story will earn their trust in return. Your story has made you the leader you are; don't sanitize or hide it.

Great leaders don't appear to be made out of whole cloth. They have stories. There are triumphs and defeats along the way. There are moments of brilliance and moments of catastrophic failures. Leaders come from somewhere, and they're on a journey to somewhere. They are shaped by their experiences and influenced by the people they meet. And the more of a leader's story we know, the easier it is to follow them.

You too have a story. You have faced challenges and overcome obstacles. You have weaknesses and failings, but you also carry talent and tenacity. Those parts of your story make you a leader worth following. Transparency requires that you open up enough of your life for others to know the people, places, and experiences that have shaped you. Whether you think your story is too boring to be interesting or too full of hardship to be relatable, it has all worked together to make you the person and the leader you are. For that reason alone, your story is worth telling.

When I think of transparent leaders, one person immediately springs to mind. His name is Edward, and he leads an addiction recovery center for men near where I live. If you were to meet Edward, you'd be immediately charmed. He's handsome, speaks with confidence, and looks every inch a leader. His program achieves incredible results and has transformed the lives of countless men. He's a valued pillar of the community and a visionary who is creating a better world.

What you wouldn't know upon meeting Edward—but what he'd be the first to tell you—is that his story is one of tragic flaws and brokenness. Before becoming the executive director of the recovery center, Edward was himself a resident in the program recovering from his own history of substance abuse and addiction. But with hard work and the help of others, he has reconciled with God, his family, and himself.

You would forgive Edward if he wanted to move on and leave his past in the past—to compartmentalize that part of his life and forge a new, independent future. You would understand if he told himself that his past disqualified him from earning the respect and trust that leadership requires. But Edward is more than willing to bare the scars of his past. He's happy to stand onstage and share the painful parts of his story. He can do all this because he knows that leadership is strengthened, not weakened, by transparency. His transparency builds trust with those he leads. It inspires people not only to buy into his vision but also to believe they can be part of making it a reality.

Transparency in the Process

One of the most frustrating statements I heard as a kid was "Because I said so." Didn't you hate it when your parent made a decision you didn't like but wouldn't tell you why?

Sometimes our parents were shielding us from information we weren't mature enough to understand, but other times it was simply easier not to explain themselves.

In the past, leaders have been able to get away with "Because I said so" answers. They've been able to keep their trade secrets under wraps. They've used their positions of authority to protect themselves from being questioned about their systems and processes of leadership. I've seen leaders cast vision without allowing those who follow them to ask basic questions like, "How? How are we going to accomplish that? How are we going to pay for it? Why? Why now? Why this way?"

This style of leadership won't make it very far in the future.

The people you lead don't want to be treated like children (if you are a middle school teacher, you might be the exception here). The people looking to you for their cues don't need a parent; they need a leader. And if you want to continue to earn trust decision by decision, you must be transparent. As an aspiring leader, you have to be willing to allow people to glimpse the information and processes you use to make decisions.

Now, I realize you're not always going to be able to share every detail of your decision-making process. Sometimes you'll have to handle sensitive information. And in moments when decisions need to be made immediately, you won't always have the luxury of time to explain the process. We don't expect government leaders to make all classified information public just so Joe or Jane from down the lane can understand the reasoning behind every decision. But whenever possible, you should be as transparent as you can.

Give a clear picture of the financial situation.

Show the actual numbers.

Describe the market forces at work.

Don't be afraid to admit that you don't have all the information yet or that the data isn't conclusive.

Let people in on the emotions involved.

Tell the stories of the people you're concerned about.

Transparency proves to those who follow you that you can be trusted with what they give you: their time, money, careers, and futures.

Increased transparency can intimidate even leaders with great integrity, not because they're afraid of being caught lying, stealing, or cheating but because even the most competent leaders sometimes feel that if someone were to lift the curtain to reveal the systems and processes that sustain their leadership, they'd feel like the old Wizard of Oz who Dorothy discovered was nothing but smoke, mirrors, and some janky levers.

Allow me to alleviate some of your concerns. No leader's processes and systems are perfect. We all operate with some things duct-taped together. It's the nature of leadership. Though we work to refine our processes so that we make better decisions more efficiently and more consistently, we never get them exactly right. But transparency breeds empathy. People like to follow leaders they can relate to. And everyone can relate to imperfection.

Lean Into Vulnerability

Some of the most disappointing and least inspiring moments I've experienced as a follower have been when I saw leaders who lacked transparency and vulnerability. If we want to be humble leaders, we will have to get comfortable with vulnerability.

I know. It's paradoxical to expect someone to be comfortable with vulnerability. By its very definition, vulnerability means being in a position of discomfort. But every great leader wakes up and eats a bowl of vulnerability for breakfast! You know why? Because everything worth accomplishing in this world requires a healthy dose of vulnerability. Want to pass an exam? You might fail. Want to ask someone out on a date? You might be rejected. Want to start a new business? It might go under. Want to win a championship title? You might lose. Do I need to continue?

Every single person who has ever done anything great started off in a position of painful and terrifying vulnerability. Might you have your heart broken? Yes, but people still fall in love every day. Could your business tank without making a single dollar? Of course, but people still become successful entrepreneurs. Is there a chance you might make it all the way to the championship game and fall flat on your face? Absolutely! But the only sports documentaries worth watching are the ones about those who lost the first time and then fought back and won it on the second attempt. You know Rocky Balboa lost the first fight, right? That guy had his face pummeled by Apollo Creed for fifteen rounds and they still made six movies about him! I bet you forgot that he lost, didn't you? You're probably pulling out your phone right now to see if I'm lying. I'm not. The comeback stories are the best ones. Watching somebody put it all on the line inspires something in us that we can't quite describe. That's the power of vulnerability.

Have you ever watched a child learning to walk? The first time they pull themselves up into a standing position, their legs work about as well as a newborn giraffe's. They take a half step forward, and then they fall straight back down. But you see them pull themselves back up to try again. They'll fall. There might be a few tears, some scraped knees, and a bump or two. But they learn. They adjust. One minute they're making progress, then suddenly they seem to have forgotten what they just learned. But they keep going. And, after a while, they get the hang of it. Before you know it, they're off and running.

That's what leadership is like. You will make mistakes. I promise you that. But if you're willing to be vulnerable, you'll learn and you'll adjust. But the minute you refuse to put yourself in a position of vulnerability is the day you stop growing as a leader. Because if you're not failing, you're not adjusting, and if you're not adjusting, you're not learning. And once you stop learning, you're done.

Humble Is as Humble Does

So how do you become a leader who embraces humility? What can you do each day to foster transparency and vulnerability? You have to do what humble people do. And humble people do humble things. I want to outline four ways you can put your flawed foot forward.

1. Never Stop Taking Notes

Leaders rarely like to admit this, but there's always someone who's smarter and leading better than we are. Leadership is competitive. And it should be. The best and the brightest minds are ready to lead people into a preferred future, and they're figuring out new and better ways of doing it. If you want longevity as a leader, you need to have a pen and paper at hand.

I've gone into a few meetings where I felt like I was the smartest person in the room. I don't like to admit that. But it's a weakness that pops up every now and again. In a meeting like that, somebody with a Sharpie and a whiteboard is usually writing down what I say. But there have been more than a few times when I've had to humbly pull up the notes app on my phone to write down the truth that got dropped by the twenty-four-year-old new hire sitting in the corner. Great ideas can come from anywhere. You just have to be ready for them.

And they don't come only from young people either. I've had senior members of my team casually ask me a question in passing that was so profound I had to write it down and think about it for a few days. Humble leaders never stop taking notes.

All right, noted.

2. Never Stop Cutting Your Own Grass

As a leader, you will always have some dirty work that you don't *need* to do, but you should. As your influence increases, you will have people who want to take more and more work off your plate so you can focus on what only you can do. That's great, and you should take advantage of that. But if you don't find ways to get your hands dirty with your team, your style of leadership won't last.

The person who last served in the job I now hold is a humble leader. When he had my job, he was extremely busy. He managed a budget of several million dollars and led dozens of staff. But every week he took time to go to a local homeless shelter that our organization partners with to wash out their trash cans. I don't know that because he told me. He probably wouldn't admit to it even if I asked him. I know that because someone who worked there told me they saw him show up and do it week after week. That's humble leadership. That's someone looking for opportunities to get their hands dirty in the work of making a difference.

I'm not saying you need to wash trash cans. I'm not even saying you need to cut your metaphorical grass with a push lawn mower. Get a riding mower. I won't judge!

But find a way to remind yourself of the day-to-day work your people are doing in pursuit of your shared vision. Organize a team day. Submit your own expense report. Take out the trash. Make the calls. Visit a customer. Don't stop cutting your own grass.

3. Never Repost Tweets of Your Own Quotes

Never repost tweets of your own quotes. To be clear, I mean this in the literal sense but also as a metaphor for all it represents. If you've done this before, I can't be mad about it, but I'm a little disappointed. First of all, your tweet is already a quote from you. It has your name and picture in the upper left corner. Seriously, think about it: that's what a tweet is. No one is confused about who said it. I'm not trying to be the guy in the Progressive Insurance commercials right now, but you're becoming your parents!

Listen, you don't need to amplify your own voice. Seriously.

Clay Scoggins
@clayscoggins

You don't need to amplify your own voice.

If what you have to say is important enough, someone else will repeat it. Of course, our job as leaders is to communicate so clearly, simply, and compellingly that someone might want to retweet it. Great communication naturally cascades. When something resonates with a group of people, it gets amplified exponentially. Whether you get the credit for it or not, humble leaders care most that the message moves people, not that people recognize the who said it.

Be a leader who strives to resonate. Anything else is just an echo. And the only voice people like to hear echoed is their own.

4. Find a Good Mirror

Have you ever seen one of those shaving mirrors in a hotel bathroom? The concave type with an LED light around it? I don't care what your skincare regime is, that thing is going to show you up! I've peered into one of those contraptions and mistaken the pores on my face for a dried-out riverbed in a sandy canyon. They're anything but flattering, but they're honest.

I recommend that leaders keep one of these mirrors close by. A leadership mirror is anything that reflects back the real you. Typically, it's a person: A critic who asks tough questions. A new team member who isn't satisfied with "how we've always done things." A friend who isn't afraid to tell you when you're being a jerk. These people are precious. They're not flattering, but they're honest.

There are times when the mirror is not a person. It might be something you've written in the past. Maybe it's a personal mission statement you wrote in a journal to keep yourself accountable. Or maybe it's a nasty reply email you sent off in anger one time that you need to keep in your archive to remind yourself of what happens when you let your emotions get the better of you. Maybe it's a recording of a podcast where you described the vision for your future that you're now constantly tempted to compromise on. It could be feedback on a 360 report from your peers and direct reports. These aren't flattering, but they're honest. And leaders of the future need to keep them close by.

Great leaders value self-reflection and are willing to do the hard work of self-assessment. And since they know they don't have all the answers, they constantly listen to others. I think we all *say* we listen to others. But much of the time, when we look like we're listening, we're really just preparing our defense for the minute they stop talking. That won't work for forward-thinking leaders. When everyone is telling you that you need to change, it's always easier to believe they're all wrong than it is to do the painful work of change. But that's what sets leaders apart—their willingness to absorb feedback and act on it. Keep the mirror up.

Vulnerability as Your Leadership Strength

If the command-and-control style of leadership is not dead, it's dying. The future leader is repulsed by it. The world is changing too quickly for anyone to know exactly what to do in every situation and circumstance. The new way requires these three simple words: "I don't know." And great leaders follow up with, "Will you help me figure it out?"

If vulnerability isn't easy for you, you're not alone. It naturally puts you in a precarious and defenseless position. By admitting your weaknesses, you give someone else the ability to hurt you. But don't forget that the weaknesses you've been fighting so hard to hide are probably not secrets to others. They know about them and they're still in the ring with you. So just admit your weaknesses, invite their help, make a plan, and lead from a position of vulnerability.

Vulnerability is a muscle to be exercised. The more you do it, the stronger you'll be. Sometimes it will feel too scary and too exposing. But press on! The world needs you—imperfect, honest, willful, and humble. The most powerful version of you is the one where you're leading from your most vulnerable place!

CHAPTER 10

Success Doesn't Have to Be a Scarce Commodity

What's the difference between a good boss and a bad boss?"

This is a question I hear all the time. Many people have had bad bosses, and most people have had good ones too. But it's hard to put your finger on exactly what defining characteristics separate one from the other. No one starts out wanting to be a bad boss. Yet, somehow, some people get there.

There are plenty of defining characteristics you can point to. Good bosses tend to have a clear vision and direction, they're able to communicate both of those clearly, and they're openhanded with the work and eager to invite their employees to wow them. Bad bosses are the opposite. They tend to lead in a direction they're not entirely familiar with, they have a hard time communicating vision, and they often keep a tight grip on the work and tasks, failing to trust those around them and beneath them to do their jobs well.

But if I had to boil down the differences between good bosses and bad bosses to one thing, it would be the ability to celebrate the success of others. Let me illustrate with two vastly different made-up stories.

Billy the Bad Boss

It was two hours before an all-staff meeting when Billy reached out to one of his younger direct reports. "Hey, I meant to have this presentation done already, but I didn't get a chance to put my notes into PowerPoint. I'm going to email them to you. Can you make them into slides for me?"

This wasn't an odd request. The employee was used to helping out her boss with whatever projects popped up from time to time, so she set aside everything she had planned to do that morning and got to work. A fresh cup of coffee in her hand, she hunkered down, ready to get this presentation done and to do it well. As she started reading Billy's notes, however, she realized this wasn't just any presentation—it was focused on a project she had personally been working on for months.

At first she was excited. All Billy's notes praised the product she had made. Several slides mentioned how it had exceeded original expectations, and there were even more thoughts on how it would be beneficial to the company moving forward. She noticed that a couple of key points were missing, so she decided to go above and beyond by adding extra slides that would answer the questions she anticipated. She worked hard to make sure the presentation looked and sounded perfect. She added extra images and mock-ups of the product alongside Billy's notes, giving every ounce of effort to make this presentation shine.

Two hours later, the all-staff meeting started and Billy presented the slides he was just now seeing for the first time. The young employee sat on the edge of her seat, waiting for her work to be recognized. But Billy never mentioned her. Not once. Instead, he walked through every aspect of the new product, fielding questions by referring to the slides that had been made in anticipation of these very questions. He acted as though he had spent weeks on this product and that the presentation was something he had thrown together at the last minute. Even when someone gave a compliment on the quality of the presentation, Billy received it in stride without even a nod in the young employee's direction.

Billy didn't simply take credit for the presentation—he took credit for the product itself. Never mind that the young employee had been pitching him this idea for months before finally getting the green light. Forget that she had put in countless late nights balancing her regular workload in addition to this new project she knew would make life better for everyone.

Not a word of any of this from Billy. He finished the

presentation, dismissed the staff, and said nothing of the work his employee had done for him. She made a slow trip back to her desk, looked at the work piled up from her morning doing someone else's task, and wondered what she was doing there.

Grace the Good Boss

It was Memorial Day weekend. A young employee had been looking forward to a weekend at the lake with his family for months now. Work had been hectic, and while he was happy with what he'd done recently, he knew it was time to take a breather. There's nothing a long weekend can't fix.

So he packed his wife, two kids, and enough sunscreen to last a month into the family car, and off they went. On the drive, he got a call from his boss, Grace. It was 5:30 p.m. on Friday, so he let it go to voicemail. His wife smiled at him. This was marital bliss.

They arrived at the lake house they rented, and almost immediately the kids were doing cannonballs off the dock, the wife was unpacking, and the employee was firing up the grill. After a great night of hot dogs and hamburgers, the family woke up the next morning ready for a full day on the dock.

The employee rolled out of bed and realized he had five more missed calls from his boss. This wasn't typical of his boss, who usually placed a high priority on family, so he decided to call her back. When his boss answered the phone at 7:30 on Saturday morning, he knew something ws wrong.

"Hey," Grace said, "I have some bad news. That client we've been working with for the past few months is about to cancel their contract. I know it's a holiday weekend, but I need you here to help fix this."

He explained that he was already at the lake but that he brought his laptop and could help for a few hours. "But that's all I can do. My wife and kids have been looking forward to this weekend all month, and I promised them a ride on the boat this afternoon."

"No problem," Grace replied. A few hours later, the employee had made his contribution to the team effort and spent the rest of his weekend at the lake, enjoying family time with his phone off.

The next week, the employee walked into work to find an envelope on his desk with his name on it. Inside was a letter from his boss that read, "Thank you so much for taking the time to work this weekend. I appreciate your effort and am glad to say the client has stayed on with us. Couldn't have done it without you."

He almost laughed to himself. He had refused to come in on a Saturday and had offered only a few hours of support, and yet he was still being thanked. Grace hardly owed him any of her gratitude. If anything, he should be apologizing for not being more of a team player. But this note communicated the opposite.

He sat down, opened his email, and set out with renewed energy and determination to see just how much he could get done today.

Giving Credit and Sharing Success

You don't need to read a chapter on employee appreciation. Literally thousands of internet articles talk about "Ways to Show Your Employees You Care." And that's great. If you're looking for year-end gifts to give your staff, definitely check out those articles.

But what I want to look at here are the underlying motivations that drove Billy the Bad Boss and Grace the Good Boss. There is a subtle difference in the way they responded to the hard work of their employees. One of them said, "Your success is a threat to my success." The other said, "Your success is my success." The former sees success as a scarce resource; the latter attitude comes from an abundance mentality.

When we're working within the same company or same team, shared success makes a lot of sense. Objectively, it's impossible to sympathize with Billy in that story. Grace went above and beyond to be a great boss, and Billy was kind of a jerk. But what about those situations when we are helping people who aren't exactly on our team? Is it possible to celebrate the success of others, even when their success doesn't directly boost our own?

For a great example of this, look at the world of Bible

translation. Currently, of the more than 7,000 languages spoken today, 3,900 have little or no access to Christian Scriptures.[1] That's a number Bible translation groups are trying to decrease. Of course, there are dozens of groups working on translating the Bible into all these languages, so you'd think they'd be pretty stiff competitors. I mean, once they've reached that number, they've worked themselves out of a job.

But that's not how these groups see it at all. Instead, they're an incredible example of what can happen when we choose collaboration over competition. When all these groups were working separately, it was estimated that the Bible would be translated into the final language in the year 2150 (which seems so far into the future that it hardly seems real). But in recent years, all the Bible translation groups have banded together to share resources and encourage one another.

Working under one roof and moving toward the same goal instead of staying fragmented has changed everything. The latest projections say the Bible will be translated into the last language that doesn't have a Bible in the year 2033.[2] That's 117 years sooner than originally projected! Think about how radical that shift is. These competitive groups sacrificed their individual advantages—particularly in fundraising efforts—in order to see everyone meet their shared goal sooner.

It is easy to see others' success as a threat to our own. We know comparison is the thief of joy, yet we still choose it anyway. We feel it when we set a New Year's goal to lose weight and then see a picture of our friend crossing the finish line of a marathon two weeks later. When we save and scrounge and finally have enough money for a down payment on a two-bedroom house, only to hear of someone buying a second mountain home. Or when we are passed over for a promotion, yet again, and then get a LinkedIn notification of a colleague who is now the president and CEO of the company they started working at just a few years ago. All these situations can take the wind out of our sails.

There is ample opportunity for us to choose envy. But comparison robs us twice. First, it steals our joy in the moment. It's hard to be happy for someone you're also jealous of. And two, it steals our joy in the future, at the time when we have experienced our own success. Even when we've hit a goal that we set for ourselves on the timetable we set for it, envy makes us wish we had set a bigger goal or achieved this one more quickly. There's no fun in that!

This isn't a new phenomenon. Sadly, failing to celebrate the success of others is one of the first mistakes humans made.

Don't Be like Cain

Something that has always interested me about the story of Cain and Abel is that Abel never says anything, at least not anything recorded in Scripture. Which is tough. He's the first person in human history to die, yet he doesn't even get a speaking role. I feel for the guy.

Anyway, if you haven't heard this story before, here's briefly what happened. Cain and Abel are the first two sons of Adam and Eve. I can only imagine how hard it was for Adam and Eve to become parents after getting kicked out of the garden of Eden. They went from a perfect lovers' paradise to a place where they had to work hard alongside their two kids, who quite clearly didn't get along. But as we read in Genesis, it appears they're trying to make the best of it.

One day Cain and Abel make offerings to God. Cain brings God some fruit. Abel brings fat portions from the firstborn of his flock. God responds favorably to Abel's offering but is indifferent to Cain's. This makes Cain so angry that he takes his brother out into a field and kills him. If you think that escalated quickly, keep in mind that this story is recounted in fewer than ten verses.

But look more closely at what happened—look at how quickly envy led to death. Abel's sacrifice was a success. Cain's was not. And instead of patting Abel on the back and saying something like, "Hey, brother, great job on the sacrifice today. What'd you do that made God like it?" Cain was angry and downcast, and he eventually let his emotions override his better judgment.

Don't we do the very same thing? I mean, we don't kill people over their success (I hope), but we let the success of others lead us toward anger and frustration. It's us versus them, and we feel we are constantly losing a game that no one else is playing.

It's hard to imagine that Abel set out to offer a better sacrifice than Cain (if he did, I doubt God would have looked favorably on it). He wasn't competing with Cain, yet when Cain realized that his sacrifice didn't measure up, it quickly *became* a competition for him.

Have you ever taken something that wasn't a competition and turned it into a fierce war in your mind? Suddenly, your friend who just got the promotion isn't only experiencing great success, but they're doing it to spite you. I once heard a younger single friend of mine say (jokingly), "It feels like all my friends are getting married at me." Doesn't the world feel like that sometimes? Like others are pointing their own successes straight at your failures?

While that may feel true, that's only our perception of reality. Abel did not give a great sacrifice to make Cain look bad. Rather, he probably wasn't thinking about Cain at all when he made his sacrifice. In the same way, for the most part, other people aren't succeeding to make you look bad. The only way you can look bad is when you choose to let their success get under your skin. You can be envious and spiteful all you want, but the only loser in that game will be you.

A quote that has stuck with me for years says, "Bitterness is like drinking poison and expecting the other person to get sick." That's what it's like when we root against the success of others. Our frustration with them—our envy, our jealousy, our whatever—isn't going to bring them down. It's only going to hurt us. In the story of Cain and Abel, Abel is the one who dies. Yet we also know he then went straight to his eternal life in the presence of God. Cain, on the other hand, spent the rest of his long life restlessly wandering the earth, never able to find a home. No one wants that.

Finding Warmth Together

I like to think of success as a campfire. It's a place for community and comradery, and ultimately, it's where we get to share in community and enjoy the presence of others.

The thing about a campfire is that once it's lit, no one checks to see whose sticks are burning. That's not how it works. No, you all gather sticks and bring them into camp with the realization that if just one catches fire, regardless of who brought it to the pit, it's a win for everyone. Each stick that ignites provides warmth for all.

Of course, when the campfire starts to burn hot, I have the option to pull out all my sticks. I could get upset when I see the fire coming from sticks others have added and grow frustrated that those flames aren't my own. But who would ever do that? In a campfire setting, that's obviously counterproductive. So why do we do this in our lives? We envy each other and choose to disengage when instead we should keep our sticks in the pit and feed off the flames of others.

When you're near a fire, you should remember that fire spreads quickly to other flammable objects. The same is true with success. It spreads to those who are eager to celebrate. Learn to see that everyone around you is working with the same fire. Success isn't scarce; it's abundant. And there is more joy in sitting around a campfire with others than there is in sitting alone, rubbing your own sticks together.

When my friends win, I win. When my coworkers win, I win. When my employees win, I win. And then when I am the one winning, we all win.

Celebrate Others

The problems of comparison, jealousy, and envy aren't going anywhere. They will remain insidious vices. Blame it on social media—where we compare our behind-the-scenes lives with everyone else's highlight reels—all you want, but even those without TikTok will always know who is experiencing what success, and we'll always compare that to our own failures. But that doesn't change the fact that the best future leaders will be ones who look for ways to cheer for other people. In a world that is growing more fragmented and siloed, the men and women who are able to reach across boundaries and give pats on the back and words of affirmation to friends, colleagues, enemies, and everyone in between are the ones who will be leading the charge.

Having an employee of the month feels like something from the past. We imagine portraits— one for every month—covering a wall, and we write it off as silly and antiquated. But I predict a return to an employee-of-the-month mentality in the future workplace. And that's because future leaders understand that celebrating success will often inspire others.

I recently talked to the employee in the Grace-the-Good-Boss story to run this chapter by him and make sure I got all the details right. I asked him what his relationship was like with that boss now, several years later. Since then, this employee has risen through the ranks and is now at the same level as his former boss. I asked if they were still friends. He responded, "I would run through a brick wall for her."

I didn't have to ask him why. It was that note, of course, and countless others over the years—the small gestures of affirmation and appreciation. I'm sure she was a good boss in a lot of other ways, but that one instance in particular stuck in his head and made him loyal forever. I asked if he had ever talked to her about the note, and he said he hadn't, which I think makes the story all the better.

This boss still has no idea what effect her simple celebrations of her employees has had on them. She is oblivious to the ease with which she acquired this man's loyalty. A kind word, an acknowledgment that you're doing a good job, that you're on the right track is often all it takes.

Leaders, consider what the future can look like. You can be the person who writes those small notes. You may be the one to change the career trajectory of those who work for you. You can be the person whose small acts of affirmation have a big impact.

Out of all the chapters in this book, this one may have the smallest ask. Go and tell someone they're doing a good job. That's it. It doesn't even have to be an employee or a coworker. Say it to your spouse, to your kids, to your friends, to your mail carrier, to anyone you see who is trying their best. Imagine the type of person you would become if someone affirmed you this way. I'll tell you who—the type of person I would want to work for someday.

You might often feel unsuccessful. But when a leader is adept at recognizing success—even in the smallest ways—and then points it out and gives credit where credit is due, success doesn't feel like such a stranger. That's how a culture is created where people aren't always fighting and bickering; they are uniting together in affirmation and encouragement, sincerely hoping for the best for those around them.

I picture this type of culture like an open mic night where everyone has incredible talent and we all can't wait for the next person to get onstage. That's a taste of what a workplace can feel like when success is celebrated from the top down. And even if you aren't leading others today, you can help create that culture in the words you use and the choices you make.

Conclusion

I'm convinced that folding a map back into its original form was Mr. Rubik's inspiration for his notorious cube. But I've always been fascinated with maps. I was the kid in the back of the car who spent more time looking at the map than I did trying to fold it back up. And my fascination with maps was always about finding the best route from point A to point B.

I love the idea that there is a "best way." Even as I'm writing this, I'm partially distracted as I try to find the best route from Westminster, South Carolina, to Branson, Missouri. Surely there is a route that is both fast and will induce the least amount of car sickness in our five little munchkins.

There may not be a "best" route to get to the future you want for your life and your leadership. You're smart enough to know there are more than nine ways leadership is changing, and we both know the final destination is not crystal clear. You may have even read or heard loads of other people who have guesses about how the sand is shifting. Some of them may be right, and others, not so much.

But not knowing the "best" or "right" way shouldn't keep you from starting the engine and beginning your journey. If you want a chance of arriving where you want to go, the first and most important step is to get into the car and start moving.

That's where most people get stuck. We either wait and let the future come to us, or we move toward what we want and hope the future will be.

It's a choice between playing offense or defense. (Yes, I'm aware that defense wins championships, but not with this figurative language I'm using.) It's about being active or being passive.

Tomorrow will eventually become today, and the future *will* eventually be the present. And you can either wait and let that happen to you, or you can follow the advice of Mr. Gretzky and skate to where you think that puck is going to be.

Not everyone is excited—or even comfortable—with change. Some of you reading this are ready to skate. Others not so much. As for me, I've never been one of those "let's get back to the good old days" kinds of people. I love that the world is always changing. I'm grateful for the ways it has changed and excited for the ways it will continue to do so in the future. Change is challenging because it forces us to choose, to decide, and to act. It won't always make your life easier or simpler. More often than not, change complicates life. But you can't avoid it. Even those who ignore it, and passively take life as it comes, have made a choice.

Life tends to grow more complicated and as we journey toward the unknown future, there are two North Stars I hold on to: *identity* and *ownership* (are we allowed to have two North Stars?). As you move toward your greatest days of leadership, keep your eyes focused on these two stabilizing forces.

Why identity? Because the best way to be ready for the future is to show up as the best version of yourself. And being the best you demands that you know yourself and know who you want to be. It means coming back over and over again to the fundamental question of your identity. Remember, who you are is always more important than what you do. Knowing who you are, how you're wired, who defines your worth, and who determines your destiny will keep you from all kinds of detours and ditches.

And why ownership? Because as our world grows more complicated, we begin to think that we can't do anything to change it. We naturally tend to accept life as it comes to us and grow cynical or even despair of making choices that matter. We fail to hold onto the locus of control, letting our lives be dictated by circumstances or the choices of others—forces outside of us. Ownership means holding onto that locus of control and believing that your choices really make a difference, no matter how small they may seem. When you keep this inside yourself, you're making sure that you are staying focused on what you can control. As the circumstances of life try to control you, constantly remind yourself that you are in charge of how you will respond to them. Of course, there will be traffic along the way. There will be those who freak out in the inclement weather. But keep your eyes fixed on your steering wheel, your own speed, and your own route. Mind your own biscuits and life will be gravy.

The future will be here as soon as tomorrow, and with every second that passes, we are one tick of the clock closer. None of us can know with certainty what the future will look like, but we can keep our eyes fixed on who we are and what we can control. This will ensure that we're in the best shape possible when we finally arrive.

Until then, safe travels. And don't worry about folding the map.

Notes

Chapter 1: A New World Order

1. Nancy Hass, "Earning Her Stripes," *Wall Street Journal*, September 9, 2010, https://web.archive.org/web /20100911195704/http://magazine.wsj.com/features/ the-big-interview/earning-her-strips/.
2. Angela Ahrendts, "How to Unite a Team," May 12, 2020, *Masters of Scale* with Reid Hoffman (podcast), 32:02, https://mastersofscale.com/angela-ahrendts/.
3. Ahrendts, "How to Unite a Team."
4. Jeff Desjardins, "How Much Data Is Generated Each Day?" *World Economic Forum*, April 17, 2019, https://www.weforum .org/agenda/2019/04/how-much-data-is-generated-each-day -cf4bddf29f/.

Chapter 2: You Don't Have to Know It All to Start Leading

1. Quoted in Andrew Fiouzi, "When Did It Become Impossible to Say, 'I Don't Know'?" *MEL*, 2020, https://melmagazine .com/en-us/story/when-did-it-became-impossible-to-say-i -dont-know.
2. Quoted in Fiouzi, "When Did It Become Impossible?"
3. Quoted in Fiouzi, "When Did It Become Impossible?"
4. Quoted in Stephen J. Dubner, "Why Is 'I Don't Know' So

Notes

Hard to Say?" in *Freakonomics* (podcast), January 4, 2012, 17:08, https://freakonomics.com/podcast/why-is-i-dont -know-so-hard-to-say-a-new-freakonomics-radio-podcast/.

5. Quoted in Dubner, "Why Is 'I Don't Know' So Hard to Say?"

6. "What Followers Want from Leaders," Gallup, January 8, 2009, https://news.gallup.com/businessjournal/113542 /what-followers-want-from-leaders.aspx.

Chapter 3: Even the GOATs Will Have a Coach

1. Joel Beall, "How Butch Harmon Has Helped the Best," *Golf Digest*, October 23, 2017, https://www.golfdigest.com /story/how-butch-harmon-has-helped-the-best.

2. Kevin Kelly, *The Inevitable: Understanding the 12 Technological Forces That Will Shape Our Future* (New York: Penguin Random House, 2016), 10–11, emphasis added.

Chapter 4: Leaders Never Fail—They Just Have Loads of Expensive Learnings

1. *The Last Dance*, episode 3, directed by Jason Hehir, aired April 19–May 17, 2020, on ESPN, https://www.netflix.com /title/80203144.

2. "I'm Telling You for the Last Time," directed by Marty Callner, written by Jerry Seinfeld, aired August 8, 1998, on HBO.

3. Carol S. Dweck, *Mindset: The New Psychology for Success* (New York: Penguin Random House, 2006), 112.

4. Alberto Savoia, *Pretotype It: Make Sure You Are Building the Right* It *Before You Build* It *Right* (self-pub., 2011), https://www.pretotyping.org/uploads/1/4/0/9/14099067 /pretotype_it_2nd_pretotype_edition-2.pdf.

5. *General Magic*, directed by Sarah Kerruish and Matt

Maude (San Francisco: Spellbound Productions, 2019), https://itunes.apple.com/us/movie/general-magic /id1458835312.

Chapter 5: Be Aware of Your Weaknesses but Intimate with Your Strengths

1. Andreas Steimer and André Mata, "Motivated Implicit Theories of Personality: My Weaknesses Will Go Away, but My Strengths Are Here to Stay," *Personality and Social Psychology Bulletin* 42, vol. 4 (April 2016): 415–29, https:// www.researchgate.net/publication/298733083_Motivated _Implicit_Theories_of_Personality_My_Weaknesses_Will _Go_Away_but_My_Strengths_Are_Here_to_Stay.

2. Michelle McQuaid, "Ten Reasons to Focus on Your Strengths," *Psychology Today*, November 11, 2014, https:// www.psychologytoday.com/us/blog/functioning -flourishing/201411/ten-reasons-focus-your-strengths.

3. Quoted in "The Reach Records Story with Lecrae and Ben Washer," interview by Henry Kaestner, *Faith Driven Entrepreneur* (podcast), October 13, 2020, https://www .faithdrivenentrepreneur.org/podcast-inventory/episode -127-lecrae-ben-washer.

4. Dan Allender, *Leading with a Limp: Take Full Advantage of Your Most Powerful Weakness* (Grand Rapids: Zondervan, 2008), 3.

Chapter 6: Get the Right People on the Bus . . . and a Few Who Aren't So Right

1. Jim Collins, *Good to Great: Why Some Companies Make the Leap . . . and Others Don't* (New York: HarperCollins, 2001), 78.

2. Collins, *Good to Great*, 13.

3. Richard Bejtlich, "Steve Jobs Understands Team Building,"

TaoSecurity (blog), October 30, 2010, https://taosecurity. blogspot.com/2010/12/steve-jobs-understands-team -building.html.

4. Rosa Parks, *Rosa Parks: My Story* (New York: Puffin, 1999), 116.

5. The Arbinger Institute, *Leadership and Self-Deception: Getting Out of the Box*, 2nd ed. (San Francisco: Berrett-Koehler, 2010), 105.

6. Doris Kearns Goodwin, *Team of Rivals: The Political Genius of Abraham Lincoln* (New York: Simon & Schuster, 2006), 280.

7. "Transcript of the Proclamation" (January 1, 1863), National Archives, last modified May 5, 2017, https:// www.archits.gov/exhibits/featured-documents /emancipation-proclamation/transcript.html.

8. PM Editorial, "Diversity Drives Better Decisions," People Management, October 23, 2017, https://www .peoplemanagement.co.uk/experts/research/diversity -drives-better-decisions#gref.

9. Nassim Nicholas Taleb, *The Black Swan: The Impact of the Highly Improbable* (New York: Random House, 2010), 63.

10. Doug Andrew, "Who's to Blame? 94% Chance It's a System Failure, Not You," Mission.org, April 16, 2018, https:// medium.com/the-mission/whos-to-blame-94-chance-it -s-a-system-failure-not-you-26396b2b3811.

Chapter 7: You Have to Give Trust to Be Trusted

1. Liz Stevens, "Do Flexible Work Schedules Work?" Best Money Moves, April 2, 2019, https://bestmoneymoves.com /blog/2019/04/02/do-flexible-work-schedules-work/.

2. Rachel Pelta, "FlexJobs Survey: Productivity, Work-Life Balance Improves during Pandemic," FlexJobs, September 21, 2020, https://www.flexjobs.com/blog/post/survey

-productivity-balance-improve-during-pandemic-remote
-work/.

3. "What Employees Really Want from the Future of
Work," McCann Synergy, February , 2020, https://www.
mccannsynergy.com/what-employees-really-want-from
-the-future-of-work/.

4. Dave Ramsey and Rachel Cruze, *Smart Money, Smart
Kids: Raising the Next Generation to Be Smart with Money*
(Nashville: Ramsey Press, 2014), 199.

Chapter 8: Conflict Never Gets Easy, Goes Away, or Feels Great

1. *The Office*, season 4, episode 3, "Launch Party," directed
by Ken Whittingham, written by Greg Daniels, aired
October 11, 2007, on NBC, https://www.imdb.com/title
/tt1031470/?ref_=ttfc_ql.

2. Douglas Stone, Bruce Patton, and Sheila Heen, *Difficult
Conversations: How to Discuss What Matters Most* (New
York: Penguin, 2010), xxvii.

3. Julie Lythcott-Haims, *How to Raise an Adult: Break Free
from the Overprotecting Trap and Prepare Your Kid for
Success* (New York: Henry Holt and Co., 2015), 6.

4. Tim Elmore, *Generation iY: Secrets to Connecting with
Today's Teens and Young Adults in the Digital Age*
(Atlanta: Poet Gardener Publishing, 2015), 26.

5. Elmore, *Generation iY*, 26.

6. Greg Lukianoff and Jonathan Haidt, *The Coddling of the
American Mind: How Good Intentions and Bad Ideas Are
Setting Up a Generation for Failure* (New York: Penguin,
2018), 7.

7. Ryan Holiday, *The Obstacle Is the Way: The Timeless Art of
Turning Trials into Triumph* (New York: Penguin, 2014), 7.

8. Holiday, *Obstacle Is the Way*, 3.

Notes

Chapter 9: The Strongest Leaders Will Lead with Vulnerability

1. Jim Collins, "Level 5 Leadership: The Triumph of Humility and Fierce Resolve," *Harvard Business Review*, January 2011, https://hbr.org/2001/01/level-5-leadership-the -triumph-of-humility-and-fierce-resolve-2.
2. Rick Warren, *The Purpose Driven Life* (Grand Rapids: Zondervan, 2012), 149.

Chapter 10: Success Doesn't Have to Be a Scarce Commodity

1. "Our Impact," Wycliffe, accessed June 11, 2021, https:// www.wycliffe.org.uk/about/our-impact/.
2. Jonathan Sprowl, "A Bible for Every Language," *Outreach*, April 30, 2019, https://outreachmagazine.com/features /global/42457-a-bible-for-every-language.html.

How to Lead in a World of Distraction

Four Simple Habits for Turning Down the Noise

Clay Scroggins

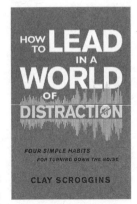

It's time to replace inner chaos with an emotional awareness that will maximize your influence and result in a calmer, less stressful, and more fulfilling life. While many leaders train themselves on how to tune-out external distractions that keep them from being productive, they remain deaf to the inner desires and emotions churning beneath the surface.

In this follow up to his bestselling book, *How to Lead When You're Not in Charge*, Clay Scroggins describes spiritual disciplines and tangible daily steps to help you incorporate four noise-cancelling habits into your daily life: Finding simplicity, speaking to yourself, getting, and pressing pause. By embracing these habits—business, church, and ministry leaders will be able to identify and understand their emotions and develop a calm and effective leadership style.

Available in stores and online!

New Video Study for Your Church or Small Group

If you've enjoyed the book, now you can go deeper with the companion video Bible study!

In this six-session study, Clay Scroggins helps you apply the principles in *How to Lead in a World of Distraction* to your life. The study guide includes video notes, group discussion questions, and personal study and reflection materials for in-between sessions.

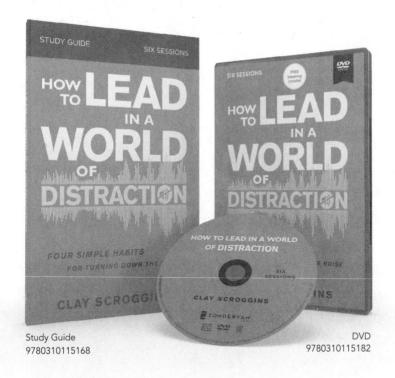

Study Guide
9780310115168

DVD
9780310115182

Available now at your favorite bookstore,
or streaming video on StudyGateway.com.

How to Lead When You're Not in Charge

Leveraging Influence When You Lack Authority

Clay Scroggins

Are you letting your lack of authority paralyze you?

One of the greatest myths of leadership is that you must be in charge in order to lead. Great leaders don't buy it. Great leaders lead with or without the authority and learn to unleash their influence wherever they are.

With practical wisdom and humor, Clay Scroggins will help you nurture your vision and cultivate influence, even when you lack authority in your organization. And he will free you to become the great leader you want to be so you can make a difference right where you are. Even when you're not in charge.

Available in stores and online!

How to Lead When You're Not in Charge Study Guide with DVD

Leveraging Influence When You Lack Authority

Clay Scroggins

One of the greatest myths of leadership is that you must be in charge in order to lead. Great leaders don't buy it. Great leaders lead with or without the authority and learn to unleash their influence wherever they are.

With practical wisdom and humor, author and pastor Clay Scroggins will help you nurture your vision and cultivate influence, even when you lack authority in your organization. And he will free you to become the great leader you want to be so you can make a difference right where you are. Even when you're not in charge.

In this six-session video study, Clay explains what is needed to be a great leader—even when you answer to someone else.

Sessions include:

1. The Oddity of Leadership
2. Lead Yourself
3. Choose Positivity
4. Think Critically
5. Reject Passivity
6. Challenging Up

This pack contains one study guide and one DVD.

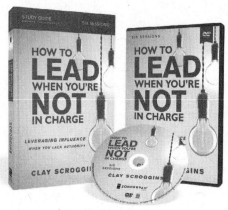

Available in stores and online!

Ready for a next step?

Follow Clay or join his email list for more insights on the future of leadership.

ClayScroggins.com

 Twitter: @ClayScroggins

 Instagram: @ClayScroggins

 Facebook: @ClayScrogginsAuthor